Late Discoveries

An Adoptee's Quest for Truth

Susan Bennett

2011
FITHIAN PRESS, MCKINLEYVILLE, CALIFORNIA

The names, locations, and other identifying details of many family members in this book have been changed out of respect for their privacy.

The interior design and the cover design of this book are intended for and limited to the publisher's first print edition of the book and related marketing display purposes. All other use of those designs without the publisher's permission is prohibited.

Cover photo: Hayden M. Bennett

Published by Fithian Press
A division of Daniel and Daniel, Publishers, Inc.
Post Office Box 2790
McKinleyville, CA 95519
www.danielpublishing.com

Distributed by SCB Distributors (800) 729-6423

LIBRARY OF CONGRESS CATALOGING-IN-PUBLICATION DATA
Bennett, Susan, (date)
  Late discoveries : an adoptee's quest for truth / by Susan Bennett.
     p. cm.
  ISBN 978-1-56474-513-2 (pbk. : alk. paper)
  1. Bennett, Susan, 1964- 2. Adoptees–United States–Biography.
  3. Birthmothers–United States–Identification. I. Title.
  HV874.82.B46A3 2011
  362.734092–dc22
  [B]
                     2011005184

To My Mother

Contents

A section of photographs follows page 98.

Late Discoveries

The Third Trimester

"Childbirth is more admirable than conquest, more amazing than self-defense, and as courageous as either one."

—*Gloria Steinem*

FOR A FRESHLY GRADUATED high school student, the future holds great possibilities—unless you're Kathy Bardlow and seven months pregnant. Even though she had plans and tried to will the trouble away, she couldn't hide her growing belly and, whether she liked it or not, a baby was on the way.

The adoption agency received a call from Mrs. Nancy Bardlow on October 4, 1964, requesting services on behalf of her daughter, Kathy, who had just turned eighteen the week before. Mrs. Bardlow also inquired about housing, a place where her daughter could live before giving birth. While they knew of a maternity house in the Bardlows' hometown of Phoenix, one in Tucson was preferred because the city was smaller and, frankly, farther away. Mrs. Bardlow urged the out-of-town recommendation, claiming doctor's orders for her daughter's well-being and mental state.

"There's a chance Kathy might change her mind, or her boyfriend might bother her," Mrs. Bardlow explained.

So the agency made all of the arrangements and Kathy was placed in a Tucson maternity home on October 17, 1964.

It was a warm fall morning when David Bardlow and his

daughter pulled into the parking space in front of a modest brick house. Kathy had sat quietly for the entire two-hour ride, but once her father shut off the engine she wailed and sobbed, much like an overheated, gurgling radiator. He sat still, focusing straight ahead and not reacting.

"Daddy, I'm so sad for my baby." She leaned forward, cradling her full belly. Tears dotted her gray-blue dress and she blubbered, "I don't want to do this. I don't want to live here. Please, Daddy...." Her body shook and her eyes pleaded for mercy as all the grief and fear she'd been holding poured out in front of her father. Yet he remained steadfast.

"Kathy, you know I have to get back. Your mother's waiting for me and I have a lot of chores on Saturday. It's my only day to work around the house," he calmly explained, resting his hand on her shoulder. He pulled a red handkerchief from his front pocket and handed it to her. "Now wipe your face and I'll get your things. Let's go on in."

Bam! The car shook as he slammed the door. Kathy felt that her own father didn't care about her situation, or the new life growing inside her. *He closed the door on me,* she thought. *Nothing I say matters at all.*

Kathy trembled and pictured herself walking away, maybe into a new life or maybe into traffic. Then she remembered what her mother had told her just as she left the house. "Before you know it you'll be home for Christmas, and there will be presents under the tree for you, from Santa. Focus on that day, Kath."

As she made her way up to the house, her feet grew increasingly heavy with each step. She climbed the stairs hesitantly, refusing to speed her pace, even at her father's urging. As she topped the last stair, her eyes raised to meet the cloudy kaleidoscope of color. *Welcome,* she read. *Huh.*

The large front door was made entirely of stained glass, with its gaudy salutation front and center. The block letters that spelled out *Welcome* were a soulful pale blue. It was almost as if the door understood her sorrowful journey. A floral pattern throughout the glass displayed murky, ginger-colored blooms and a russet earth. Around the outer edges were droopy crisscrossing pale green vines.

The door opened and an older woman wearing glasses with her hair pulled up in a bun motioned her inside. "Welcome to Marcus House," she said. "I'm Mrs. Baker, and I've been watching for you."

They went inside to a small office. "Please have a seat. I have some forms that need a few signatures from Mr. Bardlow."

Kathy sat right next to her father, gazing out the window while he signed the necessary forms. All she thought of was going home and seeing gifts under the Christmas tree.

Mrs. Baker looked at her. "Kathy, how are you feeling? Do you have your next doctor appointment soon?"

Kathy stared right through the woman, picturing only the family Christmas tree standing in the corner of their living room.

Her father stood, and shook hands with Mrs. Baker, and said, "Well, you have our telephone number if you think of anything else. I have chores to do back home." He patted Kathy on the arm as he walked past her.

Slam! The glass door shook and Kathy jumped. From the window she watched her father leave. He turned his back and walked away, without a wave or a smile. Her heart was like her mother's crystal vase, which she had accidentally dropped and shattered on the floor into a million sharp pieces.

Abandoned and grief-stricken, Kathy sat slumped in the chair and began to cry. She drew her knees up close to her belly and softly rocked herself.

Mrs. Baker calmly picked up a box of tissues, walked over to Kathy, and placed it on the windowsill beside her. "Dear, when you're done we have a few things to go over. I'll give you your name, and everything you'll need while you're staying with us."

Did she say name? She'll give me a name? Kathy wiped her face, sat up straight and looked at Mrs. Baker.

"Your new name will be Kay. It will be on your door, and it's written right here in your paperwork, should you forget. Always keep the forms handy on your nightstand. We expect you to be mostly quiet, but if you need to use your name, you use Kay."

"I have to use a different name? Why?"

"It's for your own protection, dear. After this is all over, no one will ever know you were here. Only a sad girl called Kay was here; Kay made bad choices, Kay got into trouble."

Kathy heard once more how she was bad and she was nothing but trouble, just as her mother had told her. "Bad girls get their names changed, I get it," she said out loud.

Mrs. Baker continued cheerily, "Let me call and make sure your room is ready. Then I'll show you around Marcus House, Kay." She picked up the receiver.

Kathy pictured the wooden ornaments that she and her sister had painted the year before, and how they were hung at the bottom of the tree because of their durability. *When will they be decorating? When do the Christmas shows start? After Thanksgiving for sure…. Oh my gosh, I'll miss Thanksgiving.*

Kathy had always loved Christmas, and it seemed that her mother was right. The very thought of Christmas had the power to save her from the all-consuming sadness. Kathy made her mind up to always think back to what her mother had told her, "Before you know it, it will be over and it will be time to come home to presents under the tree. Just think of Christmas."

The bright spot at Marcus House was the art room. Kathy spent all her free time there, immersed in creating. She drew pictures of Christmas trees and painted them beautifully, adding every ornament and bow she could fit into the scene.

On Thanksgiving Day Kathy grudgingly ate, thinking only of the art room. This was the one place she could focus and do what she loved. After picking at her food, she excused herself and went to paint. Kathy created enchanting holiday scenes as her imagination took flight. But now she placed her Christmas into a family room with a mom, a dad, and a baby.

"Kay, you can't stay in there all night. You're on dish-drying duty," the house mother yelled into the art room.

For Kathy, Thanksgiving had always been about family. But at Marcus House she never received one piece of mail, not even a telephone call. *They must have celebrated without me,* Kathy thought, as the holiday came to an end.

Mrs. Baker was right—Kathy was gone, and her family had no connection with *Kay* at all. One day she hoped to have her own family, and never have to live as *Kay* again.

Introduction

---

*"Life is like a roller coaster with thrills, chills,
and a sigh of relief."*
— Susan Bennett

As I LOOK IN THE MIRROR, the face of concern gazes back at me. With a furrowed brow it softly speaks to me. *Orphan.* The one word that has taken up residence inside of me, in multiple mutated forms. Yes, I am an orphan. However, the word slides off my back the same as all the other silly childhood names tossed my way. I smile, realizing I am in good company: Edgar Allan Poe, Ella Fitzgerald, Faith Hill, and James Michener were all orphans. And of course, it wouldn't be right if I didn't mention Little Orphan Annie.

To better present my story, with its skyscraper highs and bottom-of-the-barrel lows, a brief family portrait is necessary.

I came into this world with these words being echoed in the space around me: "Sorry, sorry—I am so sorry." The hospital was in a small town in southeastern Arizona, and it was 1964. The medical facility served as a common drop-off point for parents of pregnant teens trying to sequester their family shame. Just two hours away from the growing metropolis of Phoenix, it was the perfect hideout. It would take forty-four years before I would learn of my somber beginning.

Three weeks after my birth, I arrived at an apartment to begin life with my new family. My parents, Glenys and Robert, were forty-four and forty-six years old respectively. My brother, Robert, was five, and we all lived together with my grandparents, Dan and Doris.

Growing up I was close to my grandmother—often stuck to her side or at least following her shadow. That behavior is not unusual for most families; however, adults who would just as soon not be bothered by a small child dominated my childhood. My parents and grandfather believed children should be seen and not heard.

I believe everyone must have loved me; I simply didn't feel their love and rarely heard the words "I love you." My grandmother, on the other hand, loved me with her smile, her touch, and her kind ways. I adored her, and she loved her little sidekick. She was the one who taught me the most important things, like how to read tea leaves, and how to pick out the best chocolates from the See's box, carefully avoiding the icky maple ones. She lived boldly, wearing her Welsh heritage like Superman's cape, adorned with bright folklore knit and trimmed in superstitions.

While doing dishes one day, I dropped a fork and she lowered her voice in a mysterious way and said, "Ahh…you know what this means, don't you, Susie? Go—quick now, watch for a visitor."

Startled at first, I picked up the fork and we peeked out from the kitchen, watching the front door, for according to the fork and my grandmother, a visitor was soon to arrive.

My grandmother was wildly entertaining with enigmatic stories, while her kind nature gleamed like the warmth of the morning sun on your face. She captivated my spirit, creating a timeless connection between us. And for as long as I can remember, I called her "Mom," just as my mother did. Mother was always "Mother," but my grandmother was "Mom."

My brother Bob was great. As a child I looked up to him like a star in the sky. He was hilarious and amusing; actually, he still is to this day. I cherish having him in my life, and especially having had him in my childhood. I loved him so much and went along with anything he wanted to do—playing boys' games like Stratego and Battleship, eating an entire pack of bubble gum all at once, and even playing football. Bob arranged things so we played foot-ball in the narrow hallway, and I was completely unaware of the impending danger and what it meant to be tackled. A small and simple quarterback, I was sacked in every play, but I idolized Bob and loved whatever we did together. It didn't matter in the slight-est that he was five years older.

"Almost six years older than you," he told me early on. "I'm five years and ten months older, and that's closer to six years older than five." He was precise, too.

Bob really was my best friend as a child. He didn't even seem to notice that I had a purple birthmark covering my chin. The neighbors and relatives who'd stop by to visit my folks always in-quired about my chin, and my mother went along with whatever assumption they posed. Why, it could have been a rash, a Kool-Aid stain, or my absolute favorite, that I had been kissing all the boys. Those visits sent me to my room with a fit of the sulks. I couldn't understand why she didn't tell them the truth and point out my pretty blue eyes or silky pale blonde hair.

Eventually, I turned the chin issue into a race. Whenever I no-ticed a visitor approaching our door, I'd rush into my room before they even reached out to ring the bell. But my brother, he made no remarks, ever. In fact, I cannot recall even one time where he mentioned my chin. Oh, he did have embarrassing names for me that mostly rhymed with Suzie—monikers like "Oooey," "Oos-nay," and "Tudie." But then, to be unique he came up with the queen of all nicknames, "Girdle." Why, who wouldn't be proud of that? Bob and my grandmother, "Mom," were my world until I was thirteen.

It was 1978. Both of my grandparents died that year, Bob got married, and I was left with my parents to grieve and try to carry on. My mother was devastated, her heart flattened by the loss of her mom and dad, just two weeks apart from one another. My grandmother had a stroke, and my grandfather simply couldn't live without her and quickly willed himself to heaven. They had been a team, my mom and her parents, an incredible trio; and now two thirds were gone.

The ones left behind — my mother, my father, and I — tried
to move on, but we fought and argued. Our newly defined relationship was strained. I missed my brother and my grandparents,
especially "Mom." Sadness filled our house like a dense fog that
twisted and turned me around. We were all grieving, but in different ways. It was as if love had left the building. I was lost and
empty and I couldn't navigate without it. To my mother, I was an
annoyance. And in the eyes of my father, I did everything wrong.
I entered high school that year deep in grief, with no real friends,
and a big birthmark on my chin.

Against my mother's wishes, I "found" some make-up to cover my birthmark. Then I started to figure out how to get friends.
They were mostly boy friends, and girls who were trouble, but
the fog lifted for me, and my world filled with wonderful, much-
needed attention. I was supposed to wait until I was sixteen to
date boys, but attraction felt awfully close to love, and I liked it.
So I used make-up, dated boys with no parental interference, and
life was good. At least, as good as it could be.

I was spellbound with my social life and took little notice of
academics. With no direction, guidance, or support from home,
I found trouble easily. It came primarily in the form of stealing,
alcohol, and sex. A friend taught me how easy it was to slide a
bracelet off a rack and right into my pocket. It was indeed a helpful skill at Christmas, allowing the "attention seeker" in me to
give gifts to my friends.

Getting alcohol was effortless; thanks to my parents I had a
liquor store in my house. With their early bedtime of nine p.m.,
there was plenty of time to "shop" the night before an event. All
my school friends loved me on Friday nights — I had the thermos
of vodka or whiskey, and by the time the dance started, we were
all flying high.

Sex was a byproduct of attention; you can *never* have too
much attention and high school boys can never have enough sex.
It was the late 1970s, early 1980s and that was my socially acceptable life as a teenager looking for love. My mother seemed un-

concerned, even remiss when it came to me. But after all, she was now two-thirds less of a person.

Now, I have to mention that throughout high school I did have friends who weren't like me. They were the good kids. Not all the boys wanted just one thing, and not all the girls were attention-seeking fiends. I battled trying to find who I was, and where I fit in best. My thoughts and emotions were erratic and so was my behavior. This condition lasted through my high school years, right up till graduation day.

That day it all changed when I met someone special. He was in line next to Lisa Bender, my best friend, in the B section, and I was at the end in the W's.

I still think of graduation morning as the morning I met Mike Bennett. After we finally made it through the practice graduation walk, Lisa introduced me to her neighbor in line. Instantly I felt something different, joyfulness. I knew who he was—I'd had classes with him—but I'd never stood face-to-face looking into his eyes. I kept staring and he kept staring. It wasn't long (two days) until we had our first date. The second date we went out to eat and found ourselves staying up half the night talking, sitting in his car. After a few weeks, I met his parents and then he met mine, both sides seeming very agreeable to us as a couple. For the first time I felt at peace.

Mike was the smartest, most intriguing person I had ever met. He oozed personality and charm, but mostly he made me laugh and I loved being around him. When we were together, I was happy.

"I'm not sure if you've noticed or not," I said to Mike, "but I have this birthmark on my chin?" We were sitting face-to-face in the back seat of his 1972 Lincoln Continental. "It's called a port wine stain, and I cover it with heavy make-up."

Mike reached out and gently began to rub my chin with his thumb. "Cool, I can't wait to see it." He said it without hesitation, and that was it for me. Mike was the greatest, and I fell in love because he really loved me, chin and all.

After a year and a half we were married and I could not have been happier. Mike was a lot like my brother in many ways, but it was his heart and the deeply felt connection that bonded us. No, I wasn't pregnant, and we weren't forced into marrying. We truly loved each other. And frankly, in hindsight, I can see that God knew what He was doing when He brought us together. He had a spectacular plan.

Just five months after walking me down the aisle, my dad fell and broke his hip. I knew when I got the phone call from my mother that everything was about to change—again. He had bone cancer and passed away within a few months. It was heart-breaking to watch his rapid decline and witness my mother act harshly towards him in his final days. I had just turned nineteen and I was flat-out confused. It was a difficult time for my mother and I had no idea how to deal with any of it—my feelings or her feelings.

I wanted so badly to be close to my mother and forge a new relationship, but we really didn't know one another and we both found our time together difficult. By now, Mother was mostly an angry woman who felt utterly alone. She complained about not having any friends, but she was never able to be a friend. A few longtime friends, now simple pen pals, knew nothing of her sadness. Her disappointment would grow and continue for years. I loved my mother and greatly respected her; however, it was a problematic relationship.

Loneliness gripped her like thick pneumonia, squeezing her heart and closing it off. And those she loved most she repelled with bitterness and a foul mood.

"I'm so damn lonely," she often grumbled. "Nothing in this house moves unless I move it."

But everything wasn't bleak! There were many joyful moments in my mother's life. Once she started vacationing to her homeland and reconnecting with her family from Wales, Mother became brighter. It took a few years of coaxing by her cousins, but once she embraced the transatlantic flight she was in a new happy routine. She began writing honest letters to her family and found new pen pals with whom she kept in touch for many years. Her trips to Wales occurred every other year and lasted for a month at a time. Thankfully, these wonderful holidays blessed my brother and me as well. For a good three months afterwards, Mother was still on cloud nine, happier and more pleasant than usual. It was a needed respite for her and for us all.

She was challenging on many levels, but Mother loved and needed me, especially when she was much older, and that fed my emotional side. Through upset and even annoyance, her requirements were like a habit that I couldn't deny. Mother touched the part of me that longed to be wanted, no matter what the cost. Negative, even sometimes destructive attention is still attention, after all. It doesn't matter if you're fifteen or forty.

I loved my mother very much, and deeply mourned her loss in 2008. From diagnosis to passing, her enraged cancer took only two short months. Even after learning that she was not my biological mother, I gave her all my love and efforts and put the secrets and lies aside. Mother, in her final days, needed me in a pure, primal way, and I know she passed away feeling grateful for everything I had done. She felt the same gratitude toward my brother as well. I was her adopted daughter, as revealed by a DNA test result, but she never knew or felt anything other than love and respect from me, her daughter. It wasn't until after she was gone that our genetics began to weigh on my heart.

This experience, along with the many discoveries of family, old and new, has been an incredible ride with revelations, shock, tears, and fears. Learning what it is to be a Late Discovery Adoptee has been enlightening and amazing. Seeking the truth can be exhausting. Dealing with sometimes unsavory people is mind-boggling, yet even wildly entertaining. I promise that you won't be bored or disappointed on this ride—but you'd better buckle up and hold on.

Things may get a bit bumpy.

CHAPTER 1

Our Book

---

*"Each thought that is welcomed and recorded is
a nest egg by the side of which more will be laid."*
—Henry David Thoreau

"LA LA LA LA, LA LA LA LA, *Lah, Lah, Laaaaaa.*" She sang a lovely, swooping melody ending in a long, low note. A sweet, small
dance accompanied this song, no matter where she was or what
she was doing. This day however, she was sitting in her spot on
her favorite blue couch, describing to me how her dance should
be depicted on the front of "our book," as she called it.

My memories of her dancing are vivid, almost more real than
life itself. I don't know where it came from or remember when it
started; I only know it has always been part of my mother. I'm sure
it had been a part of her mother as well. She danced this one-per-
son box-step with her arms held high. It was silly and quirky and
completely, totally her. Most memorable was the grand finale,
in which she'd deftly bend her right leg up behind her, as if she
were about to receive the most wonderful kiss in a World War II
film. Everyone in the family knew Mother's little dance, whether
it was an elaborate version or one shortened for time's sake. She
might not have enjoyed doing it when the A/C repairman came
and her granddaughter insisted upon seeing it, but that certainly
did not stop her.

As we discussed the dancing figure for our book, I promised
that this likeness of her would be on the front cover, leg bent

gracefully behind in the final "kiss" pose. Of course, I knew instantly that my daughter Ashleigh, the artist, would draw it.

"Oh how lovely, great! Say no more," she said with raised hand when I told her about Ashleigh. "That is just perfect."

Our book was really my mother's life story, and I recorded everything that she could remember to share. It started naturally as a way to focus on heart-warming memories to get our minds off a painful reality.

Mother had always been active and lively, but for a few weeks she hadn't been feeling well. She said she couldn't "move" this muscle pain in her lower back. She was spending the summer in her cabin up north, but finally agreed to make the trip down to the valley to visit her doctor. After blood work and extensive testing, it was time for the abdominal scan. Mother returned to her cabin and I went home to the valley, where we waited several days for the results.

When the phone rang and I answered. I didn't know why Mother's doctor was calling me.

"It's not good, kiddo," he said.

With my stomach clenched in a giant knot, I walked to the sofa and sat down. "Okay. Well, just tell me what it is…"

"It's cancer, colon cancer, and bless her heart, I am amazed at how well she feels for how affected she is." He went on to explain the details and describe what he saw on the scan as well as what the consulting oncologist suggested.

My voice shaking, I asked, "Well, what do we do?"

"If it were me or my mother, I wouldn't do a thing. Your mom is terminal, and this cancer is in its advanced stage. Any treatment would probably kill her faster than if we left it alone. She'd be miserable with chemo and I just don't think she could take it, physically."

I had to ask the dreaded question. "How long do you think she has?"

"Maybe three months. No more than six. It really depends on her. Some people give up and it's a matter of weeks, but I don't see Glenys being one of those people," he said. "She may appreciate knowing the truth, so she can use the time to get her affairs in order."

As we talked for another ten minutes, he explained what would be best for Mother to eat and what to avoid, things for me to be aware of, and when to call him. He said that he had called me, knowing that his elderly patient was up north alone and that I might want to give her the news personally. He gave me his private number and told me to call if she wanted to talk with him; or we could go to his office and he would share the information and scans.

I hung up the phone and felt sick. I slumped forward and just sat there with my head hung low. Tears ran down my cheeks and dripped off my nose. My mother couldn't have terminal cancer, we had just celebrated her eighty-eighth birthday! In her birthday card, I'd written, "May this year be one of the best ever." Now it sank in—there wouldn't be another year, another birthday, or another Christmas. She'd spoken before of her fear of death or of being put in a nursing home. She'd made me promise that I'd move in with her and that she'd never be sent away. My mother was fearful of "The End" and wondered if there would be pain, and if so, what would it be like. But now, I was hurt and afraid. I sat petrified, knowing things would never be the same. My heart was breaking, shattering one realization at a time. It wouldn't be long before she was gone. Drop after drop, the tears flowed steadily, accompanied by an intense cramping pain in my gut and a dimness in my soul.

The next few hours were spent sharing the news with my husband, Mike, my brother, Bob, and my kids. When I reached Bob he was just getting on a plane, embarking on a long-planned family vacation. He was grateful that I could make the trip up to see Mother and explain everything the doctor told me. The rest of the night was a blur, and my mind was out of control trying to decide on the exact words to tell her. *I'm her daughter,* I thought. *I have to say the right thing, the right way.* By two a.m. I finally realized that I needed to get some sleep, and I turned to the comfort that has always helped me. I prayed.

"God, please give me strength to do what is best for my mother and give me the right words to say to her tomorrow," I whispered, and I buried my face into my tear-soaked pillow.

Early the next morning, Mike and I made a quiet, two-hour journey up north to her cabin. I watched the desert scenery with mesquite and saguaros change to beautiful mountains covered in pine trees. The higher elevation replaced the warm air with a cool sweet breeze. Looking deep into the forest I felt an unnerving solitude, a feeling of isolation that I wanted to keep from my mother. I was determined she not go through this alone and that she not die alone. As we pulled up, she and her two dogs came out, and as always, Mother opened the gate for us. I did not know it then, but this would be the last time she performed this welcoming gesture.

We got out of the car, and I gave Mother a hug, knowing that she would never be the same after learning what I had come to tell her. Watching as Mike gave her a tight squeeze, I could only wonder how many of those hugs remained. She was happy to see us and asked about our drive, hoping we hadn't encountered too much traffic. It was Mother's standard care and concern for us. Mike excused himself to go and pick up a few groceries so Mom and I could be alone. We went inside and sat together on the couch. She was quiet—I felt as if she knew something was wrong.

I was oddly calm and at peace as the perfect words simply came out one at a time. I shared every detail from the doctor, including his nutrition suggestions, her remaining time, and the fact that he had broken my heart with his diagnosis of her end-stage colon cancer.

Looking back on that day, I find that the specific details of our intimate conversation still burn inside like acid, and I can even now hardly spend more than a few moments remembering.

At first, my mother was calm. However, once we got past her diagnosis, she listened intently as I relayed her doctor's words, and her eyes filled with tears. I promise you, there is nothing more difficult than actually saying the words, *You only have a few months to live,* to your mother.

She stared straight ahead while I spoke. Her mouth turned down and even though I could only see the side of her face, the sadness and disappointment were louder than any words she could have said.

Then Mother turned to me. "Well, shit! I just read the other day that once you make it to eighty there's only a small chance that you'll get cancer; and I'm eighty-eight."

I thought, *There you go, you be mad. Mad is way better than sad. Yeah, I like mad; we can be mad together.*

"Why me?" Her tone deepened with anger and her voice got loud. She was angry, frustrated, and then there it was; the profound look of sorrow.

With her head down and her hands covering her face, she sat still for a minute. Then abruptly she lifted her head and said, "Ohhh...well, why not me? I just said it—I am eighty-eight and I have had a long, full life." With resolve in her voice, she added, "It had to happen sometime, I suppose."

We went on from there discussing foods she should and should not eat, and she spoke with a brighter tone. Her nutrition going forward could make a difference, and Mother wanted to stay as pain-free as possible. She didn't feel the need to call the doctor, and she definitely wasn't making the trip down to see him. In that moment she was able to think about the next couple of days and the next week, and that worked to dull the sting of her fate.

Mother did love her place up north and the weather that came with being in the mountains. And her best friend Cathy had recently moved back to town.

"I'm staying at the cabin for as long as I can. I have my friend Cathy here, and you kids will visit, end of story. That's what I want to do." Mother made her wishes crystal clear, and we respected her decisions. It was all about her happiness and comfort; that was the goal.

But her brightness lasted only about as long as her favorite James Bond movie, and then all the things in her life that she couldn't do rushed to mind. One last trip to her homeland of

Wales, seeing her youngest two grandchildren get married.... She began to think of how she might die. I could see her darken, and knew she was thinking of death.

I didn't want Mother to lose any time by being regretful. She needed to focus on the good, as simple as that may sound. I was flooded with joyful things to talk about as questions popped into my mind.

"Tell me again about the time when you and Mom and Gramps left Wales," I asked. "And how old were you?"

"Oh, you remember, I was about five, and we got on this huge ocean liner, the *Mauretania*. I remember seeing it for the first time with these four enormous smoke stacks. It was some trip, and so was my holiday that reminded me of our journey some sixty years later."

Her face relaxed, as she leaned more comfortably on the arm rest and continued. "Did I ever tell you about the time when I was visiting my cousins in Wales? We went into this pub for a quick bite to eat. I went to the back to wash my hands, and as I came out of the ladies room and walked down the hallway, I looked up and saw this huge framed painting of a large ship. And there it was — one, two, three, four big smoke stacks, and it stopped me dead in my tracks. It was the *Mauretania*. I stood there and cried. I put my hands on the painting and said, 'Oh you're here with me, Mom and Dad.' I felt my parents with me, right there in the pub."

Of course, I'd heard parts of the story before, but as I listened this time I realized that what gave my mother so much joy was her history, and her love for her family — particularly her parents.

I moved closer to her and held her hand. Quietly I asked, "Mom, I love so many things about your life, and you've done so much and gone so many places, I think we should write them all down so I'll never forget. Is that okay?"

"Oh my, lovely, that would be great!" She smiled at me, her eyes filled with tears. "I would really like that." She scooted closer and put her arm around me.

We held each other for a few minutes, crying for the sad news of the day, but also for the happy decision to write her story together. Mother saw it from the start as *our book* and we both held on to it intently, giving it focus and embracing the welcome distraction. It was to be *ours*, and Mother would happily share the plan with friends and family.

After everyone knew Mother's diagnosis, and the tears were dry, she excitedly told her friend Cathy. "My Susie is going to write down our family stories and history. We're going to cover it all. I imagine it will be a very thick book when we get done. I've been making notes on pads around the house and there are a lot of events to tell about. Did you know that my mum came from the Forest of Dean? That's where Robin Hood was from! Did you know that we took the *Mauretania* over from England? My granddaughter Ashleigh will do my picture for the front cover. It will be smashing good."

"I can't wait to read it," Cathy said. "And don't leave anything out."

It seemed like only minutes had passed, and we experienced every emotion, as if a roller coaster were rushing us through grief, confusion, sadness, and anger, then acceptance, and even joy. We ground to a complete stop, exhausted and with our hearts racing. The safety bar lifted and we stepped free. Mother may have been at the end of her life, but *our book* gave us a rose-tinted view. We lived in the moment, safe and secure, in the calm at the eye of a hurricane. The day was over and we had a plan. We would enjoy even this phase of life, one day at a time.

CHAPTER 2

The Mauretania

"To be born Welsh is to be born privileged, not with a silver spoon in your mouth but music in your blood and poetry in your soul."

—*Anonymous*

MY MOTHER'S FAVORITE STORY to tell was her journey to America. She detailed her trip across the Atlantic by recounting stories told by her parents. However, she also quite distinctly remembered several things she had experienced as a precocious five-year-old. Coming to America was clearly one of the greatest events in the lives of her and her parents, and hearing it told, rich in imagery and emotions, has turned it into a beautiful film that plays in my mind.

The *Mauretania* brought hundreds of European immigrants from Southhampton, England, to Ellis Island in the 1920s. Among the passengers arriving on August 28, 1925 were Daniel and Doris Roderick and their daughter, Glenys. She had turned five in June and her parents were in their late twenties. They knew some English, but freely they spoke Welsh. Glenys called her parents "Mum and Tad," the Welsh equivalent of Mom and Dad. The move to America changed their lives forever, cementing their family bond in a love fixed beyond place and time.

During the six-day journey, a serviceman overheard a little girl singing to herself as she played and wandered the lower deck. He spoke to the child, asking her what the song was called, but she couldn't fully understand him. With a smile and a few gestures, she told him the first line of the song, "Show me the way to go home." Glenys loved this English song she had learned from her mum and she knew this journey was taking them to a new and wonderful home.

The serviceman asked, "Please, dear, won't you come up and sing your lovely song for our first-class passengers on the upper deck?"

Glenys looked at him, not sure what to do...but then thought, *I do love to sing.*

He held his hand out and smiled, "Only one song, love."

Glenys gladly took hold, and off they went so she could sing for the crowd.

Only a week earlier Glenys had sat behind the bar of her favorite auntie's pub with her cousin Des, singing along as the adults merrily bellowed, "Show me the way to go home," the rousing new song by the popular duo Irving King.

In the pub, Glen and Des would dash out from behind the bar and sneak dribbles from shot glasses left at empty tables. They would squint their eyes together, wrinkle up their noses, and swallow hard.

"My mum said we were like little devils and wouldn't listen to a soul! Such good times with Des, Mum, and Aunt Elsie—oh so many," Mother reported with a childlike gleam in her eye.

But on the huge vessel, there were no pub tables and no cousin Des. They'd left the pub and their home country far behind. Nonetheless, the little girl knew she was headed for a bright future in America with her parents and that's all that mattered.

As they set foot upon the upper deck, the serviceman announced, "Hear now, this lovely little Welsh girl will sing us a song."

The first-class passengers gathered around to hear the little blonde girl sing. An older gent brought over a large crate and lifted Glenys up to stand on top. With her pillar-box red jacket, she was the center of attention. Glenys swelled with pride and enthusiasm as she began to sing:

"Ohhhh...Show me the way to go home.

I'm tired and I want to go to bed.

I had a little drink about an hour ago,

And it's gone right to my head."

Passengers clapped in time and tapped their toes as Glenys continued.

"No matter where I roam..."

She spread her arms wide at the audience.

"...Over land or sea or foam,

You'll always hear me singing this song—

Show me the way to go home."

Then she took a deep breath and slowly sang,

"Yes, show me our new HOME."

Folks raised a cheer and some wept. The crowd applauded for several minutes.

"Lovely, darling!" a woman in a pleated emerald dress called out as she handed Glenys a five-pound note. "Here you are, that was just lovely," she said, her eyes welling with joy.

"Oh, my, thank you!" Glenys shoved the money inside her dress pocket and patted the outside with pride. She smiled with a sparkle in her eye, pondering, *I think I may be quite famous.*

The older gent sang out, "And again—*Oh...show me the way to go home...*" His voice was deep and resonant, and punctuated with a rich Welsh accent.

They sang together, with Glenys still atop the tall crate, and everyone joined in singing the tune.

But while the celebration continued, Doris was frantic down below, searching for her precious daughter. She asked each person around her, "Have you seen my wee girl?"

Doris began to cry, "Oh I've lost my child. Where is my Glenys?!"

As she approached the steps to go up a level, she asked a laundry stewardess, "Please help me find my child. She's not down here and I'm terribly afraid that she may have gone overboard." Her forehead glistened with sweat and her legs trembled.

The stewardess put her arm around the frantic mother. "Dear, is she the adorable child entertaining the crowd upstairs?" With a warm smile she told Doris, "It's fine dear, go on up and see your daughter."

Bewildered, Doris took a few steps up and heard singing and clapping. Yes, indeed, she found her daughter at the center of attention and the choking fear was replaced by relief and then pride. The cool sea breeze helped smooth any hint of worry from her face.

Doris collected Glenys and they walked back to the stairwell amid cheers and applause. And while holding her mum's hand, Glenys turned and bowed to the crowd one last time.

The rest of the journey took place down below in steerage, where most of the lower-class passengers stayed. Quarters were cramped, but the little family of three—Dan, Doris, and Glenys—huddled together safe and secure. The smell was not pleasant and steerage lacked the fresh ocean breeze, but it was easily survivable. The singing and joyfulness on the upper deck had been a terrific reprieve mid-journey, one they would never forget. The voyage was the beginning of a new life as well as a newfound bond for the trio.

Finally, the day arrived. The *Mauretania* had completed her transatlantic journey in six days. As the morning sun warmed their backs, it shone brightly on the approaching country of America, Ellis Island, and the Statue of Liberty. Passengers packed the deck of the huge vessel, watching with excitement as the symbols of freedom and prosperity came into sight. Many had heard about Lady Liberty, but her size and beauty took everyone by complete surprise. Gasps and tears of joy spread across the deck as immigrants felt hope fill their hearts.

Even though she was only five, Glenys felt the magnitude of the moment as she saw her parents weeping. Her father held his red handkerchief bunched up in his hand with just the corner showing, allowing him to dab the tears from his cheeks.

She squeezed her mum's hand and said, "I thank *Duw*, Mum, for *darparu* us to *Ryddid*."

Mother remembered the words after all these years. What

she'd said in Welsh was, "I thank God, Mum, for delivering us to Liberty."

As my terminally ill mother sat on her couch talking about the life-changing journey and singing, "Show Me the Way To Go Home," I could see her as a child singing on the huge ocean liner. I could see the passengers on deck, the men dressed in suits, women in dresses and hats, all clapping and enjoying her. It must have been an incredible sight. Now, I truly felt the magnitude of the trip, and my heart is forever warmed knowing her profound love for that time in her life. I valued being with my mother, in that moment on the *Mauretania* and in that most precious moment next to her on the couch, writing *our book*.

CHAPTER 3

A Life in America

"The love of a family is life's greatest blessing."
—Anonymous

MY GRANDPARENTS, Daniel and Doris Roderick, were born in Wales, the United Kingdom. Daniel was born in Pontypridd, Glamorgan in 1895, and Doris, born Doris Hilda Grindle, in Treherbert, Rhondda Valley in 1898.

When Doris was three years old, she moved with her family to the Forest of Dean in Gloucestershire, England. When she was a young girl, her older brother William told fantastic stories of how their family had received aid from Robin Hood and his Merry Men. Robin Hood was a dashing young man who benevolently assisted many needy families by taking from the rich and giving to the poor. Doris tried to catch sight of him bringing food or coins to her father, but it seemed he most often visited at night. Doris always believed the stories, and hoped one day to marry a man just like him.

Seventeen years later, all her hopes and dreams came true in the form of a wonderful man named Daniel Roderick. He lived near the Grindles and stopped by to check on the family after a storm. Their eyes met when he spoke with her father about how to fix their damaged roof.

Doris was enamored with Daniel and enjoyed his company and dry sense of humor. He was as helpful as he was good looking, and they spent time together every day, whether doing chores or simply chatting in the garden. And Daniel was besotted with her. She was like nothing he had ever seen before, angelic with a pure beauty. They were over-the-moon in love and twenty heart-beats later Dan was on bended knee, proposing. Dan was better than any legendary Robin Hood, and in 1918, after a romantic courtship, they married.

The couple came from large families, each with eight sib-lings. However, the spark from these soul mates created only one shining star. This brightness in their hearts was my moth-er, Glenys Loubell Roderick, born in Treherbert in 1920. Sadly, there were complications giving birth, and Doris could never bear another child. Glenys was their only child, and she was adored.

Economic times were hard in the region and the Roderick family was poor. As Glenys grew past infancy, their situation wors-ened. The family's only income came from Dan, who worked in the Bute Merthyr Colliery, the local coalmine. After United Na-tional Collieries purchased it in 1920, production slowed and then stopped. Eventually the mine remained open only as a pumping station, and very few workers were needed. Most days Dan was sent home early, earning a small fraction of his normal weekly wage. The Rodericks were desperate, getting by solely with family handouts week by week. It was a dark irony of having little in a fertile, civilized land, but starvation or even malnutrition was not an option. They had a will to survive.

Their familiar world was being torn apart. By 1925, most of Doris's family had immigrated to the United States of America, and the Rodericks saw no other option than to follow. Dan's par-ents and young siblings had already moved to another mining community to share a home with a large family. Dan and Doris were alone in their planning and decision-making, but both knew a change was ahead. Some of the stories relayed from newly ar-rived family members made the decision difficult. There were reports of horrifying illnesses and deaths, with children being the most vulnerable.

Fearing for her health and ultimately her life in America,

Dan and Doris made arrangements to leave Glenys with a neighbor in Wales. Young Glenys had no idea, but her parents planned to leave her with the neighbor until an aunt could come to collect her and raise Glenys as her own. Only if they returned to Wales would Dan and Doris be able to reclaim their child. However, when it came time to deliver Glenys next door, the proud and loving parents could not go through with it. After many tears, they decided it was best to stay together as a family, no matter what was in their future.

My mother did not learn of the hardships in her homeland, or of her possible abandonment, until her teenage years.

As she talked about her early childhood, she put her hand up to her chest and said, "Thankfully, my folks insisted that our family remain intact. Thank God, you know? My aunt who stayed in the U.K. was a miserable woman—I couldn't stand her." We both laughed out loud and Mother added, "Miserable Nancy... they called her Nan, *ugh.*"

The Rodericks arrived in America filled with the hope of finding work and dreams for a prosperous future. They had only fled Wales because of dire economic conditions, not because they didn't love their homeland. They planned to return one day to the green rolling hills with sheep roaming throughout the countryside. Wales was their home, and the home of their ancestors.

At the time the Rodericks came, the U.S. government required all immigrants to be sponsored by an established and self-sufficient family who already lived in America. Fortunately, Doris's parents were more than willing to sponsor them, so she and her family settled nearby in central Illinois.

My mother remembered their experiences from a child's perspective. She shared stories of their simple life, which was filled with love and laughter. As a girl, she was happy, and she enjoyed school. She and her mother often sang songs as they went for long walks together. Her dad was a tease and always quick with a joke. Time with her parents was pure joy, and she was satisfied with her life. Even though there were a few hungry nights, she didn't focus on that. She proudly recounted the day when she was asked to help her mum with the shopping, not for food but rather a grand gift for her dad.

"Grab your coat, Glen. We only have a few hours to find a big surprise for your dad," Doris said in a rush.

"What's the big surprise, Mum?"

"We are going to buy something magnificent. Oh Glen, your dad will be so happy. We're getting him a radio, so he can listen to the baseball game at home in his chair."

Well that's not really magnificent, the ten-year-old thought as she looked at her mum.

"Glen, did you know your dad listens to the ball game at the neighbors'? He sneaks down the hall, squats beside the door with his ear pressed to the crack, but loves every knee-breaking minute of it. American baseball is one of his favorite hobbies. He shall have his own radio for Christmas!"

And sure enough, they found the perfect radio at Woolworth's, where they put it on layaway. With many weeks left to make payments, every spare penny went towards Dan's big surprise.

Two months later, on a crisp Christmas day, my grandfather, Dan Roderick, was moved to tears at the sight of his new Atwater Kent radio.

"I'm a rich man. I've got my radio. Thank you, my two girls, I never expected anything like this. Oh how lovely, just lovely!" he said.

Glen climbed up in his lap. "I love you, my dear Dad," she said softly and kissed his cheek.

"I'm the luckiest man in America. I cannot get over this magnificent radio just for me. Oh *Duw*, I thank you for my two girls."

"It *is* for a magnificent man, for you, my Daddy, and you are welcome."

Glenys realized her mum was right; the radio was the grandest gift. And except for a few candies and a pair of socks, it was the only Christmas gift in the house that year, but it was perfect.

As the years passed, that radio provided the family many hours of enjoyment. Sitting together next to the Atwater Kent, Glenys thought they had a great life and were the happiest family around.

Sure, some kids at school had fancier clothes and toys, but she had her parents and a deep love, and that's all she needed.

Doris and Dan's first jobs in America were in the hospitality industry, keeping a small local hotel running. Glenys was enrolled in elementary school right away, and she had already been to school for a year back in Wales. They lived in a modest apartment near the train station, which made travel easy. In the beginning, it was smooth sailing, and the Rodericks were hopeful.

Unfortunately, in the late 1920s Illinois and the rest of the country were well on the way to economic ruin. Officially, the Stock Market Crash of 1929 created the Great Depression, and everything they had tried to escape back in Wales was once more bearing down upon them. First, Dan lost his job at the hotel and was unable to find steady work. Doris was able to continue working for several more months; however, both her pay and her hours dwindled. Each parent also did odd jobs, whatever they could do in and around the neighborhood to earn money and keep the family going.

They were accustomed to rationing and getting by on very little, having done just that for years back in Wales. Thankfully, in their American community they would not ever starve. Franklin Delano Roosevelt was President, and he vowed to help everyone, the small family of three from Wales included. With newly appointed government agencies like the Federal Emergency Relief Administration (FERA) and the National Recovery Administration (NRA) and their programs, the Rodericks managed their money and food well.

Relief allowances per family in Cook County went from $29.15 in December 1932 to $33.11 in June 1934, and to $38.65 in June 1935. While those allowances hardly met most families' needs, when coupled with other programs for clothes, medical services, and CCC employment for young men, they kept many families together until things improved.

In 1935, my mother turned fifteen and felt it was time that she helped her family financially. She had already graduated high school, early by most standards, and working was the next logical step. It wasn't legal for Glenys to get a job at her age, but her enthusiasm and hard work soon landed her a job with the telephone company as a switchboard operator. On the application, she may have simply "remembered" her year of birth incorrectly.

So, five days a week Glenys and Jean, her best friend from high school, rode the train into downtown Chicago.

On payday, Glenys cashed her check and brought the money directly home. She had a great sense of responsibility. She and her parents had struggled together, immigrated together, and now she would do her part to improve the family's quality of life.

Harkening back to the great success of her dad's surprise radio, Glenys took her overtime pay to Woolworth's. Doris dreamed of an electric sewing machine, and Glenys worked hard to get it for her. She knew how pleased her mum would be, and keeping the secret was almost difficult.

Weeks later, one Saturday morning while the family sat at the table, there was a knock at the door.

"Oh, now who's this on such a lovely morning?" Doris asked.

Glenys pushed away from the table before her mother finished speaking. "I'll get it Mum, no trouble." And she raced to the door.

As the delivery man wheeled the dolly inside, Doris peeked around the corner. "What's this? Aren't you the lad from Woolworth's?" She recognized his olive-green vest right away.

"Yes, ma'am—I'm setting up your sewing machine and cabinet."

"Don't I wish it were true. I'm sure you have the wrong address, young man."

"You're Doris Roderick, right, ma'am?" he asked, smiling.

"Why yes. What...who sent this?" She ran her hand along the top of the maple cabinet.

"You've got to sign for it." The young man held out his clipboard and Doris looked at the yellow form.

Customer name: Glenys Roderick. Doris stepped back in shock.

Glenys bounced up behind her, hugged her, picked her up

off her feet, and twirled her around. "Wheee, isn't that some-thing! We have a Singer Deluxe electric model number sixty-six!" Glenys shouted.

Both women squealed and danced. *"La la la la, La la la la, lah, Lah, Laaaaaa,"* Doris sang. She went up on her toes, swirled around, held the pose and then began again.

It was the first time Glenys saw her mum sing and dance her special little jig, where she raised her leg to the back and then held the low note of the last *Laaaaaa*.

Doris couldn't have been happier with her sewing machine. It was the exact make and model she wanted. And almost every time before she sat down to sew, she sang and danced. She made tops, shorts, and dresses for them both. It wasn't long before she was able to make drapes for their single picture window, and slip covers for the furniture. Doris loved to sew.

While sharing the delightful recollection of that gift, Mother told me, "Oh my, Susie, it was wonderful. Every time she looked at her Singer, it was like we'd all received a gift—the gift of my mum. Maybe the 'Singer' inspired the *La la la* song. You never know."

Life together was special for Mother and my grandparents. Yes, early in their marriage, my grandparents talked about a large family, but their one abundant blessing made them whole. The small family of three often referred to themselves as The Three Musketeers. They were joyful and treasured one another in their new homeland of America—all for one and one for all.

CHAPTER 4

Gifts in Arizona

"No gift bestowed upon us is so precious as children. They are proof that God still loves us. They are the hope of the future."

—*James E. Faust*

THE SKY WAS CLOUDY in northern Arizona as we sat inside Mother's cabin, excited to be writing. Today's entry was about coming to this western state. We each had a cup of tea and Mother sat in her spot on the couch. Directly across from her, I waited with *our book* in hand, pencil ready. (And for some reason, for me, there is nothing like a No. 2 pencil.)

"I remember coming to Arizona on July twenty-first, and it was 121 degrees. Our car didn't have air conditioning and your dad's face was beet red. We were soaked down our backs and bottoms. Thank God, we sent for your grandparents by plane a few weeks later. It was for 'our Grampie' that we relocated here, as the intense dry heat was best for his health," Mother explained.

She often referred to my grandfather, her beloved father, as "our Grampie." She treasured him.

I admired their decision. "He did seem frail and I remember he had trouble with his lungs, but I didn't realize that the move to Arizona from Illinois was for him. That's amazing that you and Dad moved the four of you out west for Grampie's health."

"Ohhh yes, we sold things and saved before the trip and were able to buy a small home in downtown Phoenix. It had a few rental cottages on the property. In the fifties there was not a lot to Phoenix, and property was very inexpensive. We kept up the cottages and paid for our house by keeping those rented out. My job let me easily transfer to Mountain Bell—the phone company in Phoenix—and I started work the next day. Plus, your dad got a job as an insurance adjuster, and Grampie felt so good that he started Dan's Gardening. Money was no problem.

"We had an outside patio with chairs, tables, and a couple of chaise lounges. As the nights got cooler, it was a wonderful time for us and our new neighbors. We sat outside, sometimes had a few drinks, played cards, and listened to music on the radio. We truly enjoyed our new place and we all—your dad and I, Mom and Grampie—were happy and healthy. I thought it just couldn't get any better, but boy, was I in for a surprise."

"Oh no, did someone get sick?" I asked.

"No. Well, yes—sort of. At first, I thought *I* was sick. I felt run down and that went on for two weeks, so Mom insisted I see the doctor. He checked and looked at everything and then came in and told me I was pregnant. Pregnant! I couldn't get over it, Sue. We thought I'd never have a baby. The doctors in Chicago all said your dad was sterile. We'd gone for tests over the years, and they thought his sterility was from when he was in the Navy. Your dad was exposed to hazardous nuclear waste on a submarine. But, they really didn't know if it would be permanent. It didn't matter, I was pregnant… *wheeee!*"

"And there were no worries about the baby's health? Or maybe it doesn't work like that."

"No, and I felt fine once I got past the first trimester. My hair shone and my skin was bright. It was wonderful. Mom and I got everything ready and we were so excited for this baby. I think it was one of the happiest times of my life. The most unexpected, but the happiest. We thought the baby would come on Valentine's Day, but it came the day before. It was an easy delivery and when the doctor told me 'You have a son,' my heart, I swear, skipped a beat. I heard his words over and over in my head, *you have a son, you have a son.* Oh, the tears were running down my face as the nurse put him in my arms. It was un-believable."

"I can imagine how great it was with your mom there, Grampie, and Dad, too," I said. "How joyful, that little house had to have been turned on its end with the arrival of a baby boy."

Mother was animated and full of life; she recalled her feelings so easily, as if it were only yesterday. Sick? Terminally ill? What cancer? It was 1959 all over again, and Bobby had just come into the world. She told about his eyelashes, his fingers, and his perfect nose. This was a point in her life that had deep emotional meaning, but it was her connection alone. Void from the picture was my father. The stories often included details with my grandparents being present, but she didn't mention Dad very often.

"How did Dad do with a baby?" I ventured. "You know, you haven't mentioned Dad much." Maybe there was something I didn't know, and I hesitated, but then figured that under the circumstances now was the time to ask.

"Your dad really wasn't around much," she answered. "When he was, he didn't change diapers or help with the baby very often. Those were things the women did."

She gave me a quick wink, and that was it—she was done talking about my dad.

I don't know why—intuition I suppose—but I think there was a lot more to their relationship than my mother shared. She never seemed sad about it. Her life was complete, living with her folks and having her son. My dad seemed often forgotten, but it worked for them.

Without missing a beat, Mother changed the subject. With a wide smile, she moved to the edge of her seat and recalled another story.

"When Bob was about a month old, he was in his crib and I was getting ready for Mom and Grampie to come over. They lived just next door. Mom came in, calling, 'Yoo hoo, we're here!' I peeked around the corner, told her the baby was asleep, and that I was finishing up getting ready.

"Well, Mom and Grampie snuck in the baby's room to have a look. I could hear her talking to him and then all of a sudden, she yelled out, 'Glen, come quick—there's something wrong with the baby!'

"I raced into his room and saw my mother and father with their hands over their mouths. My dad looked terrified as he caught my eye. My heart jumped and I shook, thinking, *Oh God what is wrong with my baby?*

"Mom picked up Bob and turned towards me. 'Oh no, Glen, he has a horrible rash.'

"I took him and held him. Then I had to turn away in total embarrassment. 'Mom he's fine,' I said. 'I was getting ready and he needed a nap, so while I was changing him…he was so sweet and…well, I kissed him all over… and, well… I had just put lipstick on.'

"Of course, they retold that story to everyone, explaining how I'd given him a lipstick rash, and how they were just about to call the ambulance. We had a few good laughs over that one."

I don't think Mom had ever told that story in such detail or with such love in her eyes. Oh, I'd heard it before many times, but not with the emotional tone and the wide smile. We also had a good laugh right then. I can still hear her and see her face when she talked about the lipstick.

Mother went on to explain how the four of them (plus little Bob, who was about ten months old) all moved up to northern Arizona. They replicated exactly what they had done in Phoenix, but this time the rental units were log cabins. The property was large, with two small cabins to start, and a nice-sized main house. This was another endeavor in which they were all in agreement, and property was dirt cheap.

"You know, Sue, your dad was very handy and could build or fix most anything. He loved to work and wield a hammer. Grampie was very capable too, and Mom and I were there to help. We planned to live in the big house, remodel the two cabins into vacation rentals, and add cabins along the way. The Broken Arrow Lodge was a terrific venture. Bobby, as a toddler, oh boy…he loved it up there. There were animals around and a horse nearby, but his favorite thing of all was helping."

Hearing about my brother's birth, his first few months, and then his first few years at Broken Arrow Lodge made me anticipate the story of my beginnings. I knew Mother loved us both, but I also knew from as far back as I can remember that Bob was always her favorite. I figured that her first-born child seemed miraculous and extra precious, since she had believed she would never have a child. It was bearable though, since we were so many years apart in age, and he was a boy and I a girl. And, to be honest, I've always been crazy about him as well!

Life in the White Mountains was busy and everyone worked hard. Mother told about building the Broken Arrow Lodge and the bitter cold winters with several feet of snow. From October to April, the outside work for lodge owners, was unbearable, so after a few years my folks and grandparents sold and bought a home nearby that didn't require any work. My dad opened a liquor store, and things went along pretty well.

As I recorded Mother's story, I anxiously awaited any hint of my arrival. I should be entering the picture any minute now! I wanted to hear all about my lovely fingers and toes. Even a lipstick rash would be welcome. However, with her illness, small things would easily derail her. We invariably talked about something that she, Mom, and Grampie did, which was half of her favorite subject. The other half was tales of Bobby.

Finally, after a few breaks and another cup of tea, I asked about me. "Mom, how did you find out you were pregnant with me? Did you have a clue?"

"You know, it was the oddest thing; I was busy and Bobby was about five and I just had a feeling. For us to have Bobby was such a miracle because of all the hazardous work your Dad did on the submarines."

And with that, Mother recounted the story of my brother being born and how good she felt when she was pregnant. She completely avoided discussing her pregnancy while carrying me.

I interrupted. "So, did you feel really good when you were

pregnant with me also?" I wanted to know the answer. I had never heard anything about my beginning, which was an odd realization.

"Oh yeah. Do you know your brother was so enamored with you? 'She's my baby sister,' he used to tell his friends. When we were driving home from the hospital, he sat in the back seat and held you in his arms. After much discussion about your name most of the way home, he really liked the name Kimberly. But in the end, we went with Susie. We now had our two kids, Bobby and Susie."

What? That's it? That's your answer? So I asked, "You guys lived up north when I was born? Yet I was born in southeastern Arizona in a Tucson hospital. How did it work out that I was born so far away?"

"Well, we didn't like the hospital serving the White Mountain area." Mother sipped her tea and continued, "It was very dirty and small. So, we drove down to Tucson to have you. We were so lucky to have Bobby and then you popped up. That's it."

I could feel my face twist in confusion. Surely, Mother knew that wasn't going to fly just by looking at me. It was such a bare, simple explanation. Where was the wonderful story, the details about my nose and small ears—and I have such small ears, especially compared to them. Why was that supposed to be enough for me? I felt like I was ten again and the last one picked for kickball. I slumped in my seat with a long face.

No, I'm not going to give up. I asked, "Did Dad drive you to the hospital after your water broke? Were you having contractions? That had to be about a five- or six-hour drive."

"You've asked me before why you were born in Tucson, and you just were. It's how it worked out and we're not going to talk about it any more." She shuffled some papers around on the coffee table, and moved to the edge of her seat. With a scowl on her face and in a curt tone, she said, "I'm going to go lay down now."

And, that is exactly what she did. She got up, turned, and went to her room.

I just sat there—pencil in hand and *our book* on my lap. I

looked at her empty spot on the couch. I was shocked. *What had just happened?*

When I'm upset or anxious I clean, so that's what I did. Mother slept and I spruced up the place. I picked up the living room, dusted, and then made my way to the kitchen. The kitchen was the perfect place to deal with feelings, with so many things to clean. *Eureka!* There was a sink full of dishes to wash, rinse, and dry.

As I bitterly scrubbed and washed, I thought about my unusual birthplace, hundreds of miles from our home. I added the information that my brother had held me in the back seat while they decided my name. A five-year-old holding a newborn traveling by car, and it would have been for many hours. I'd often thought my birth circumstances were a bit odd, but now it was obvious that something was not right.

Suds were rinsed away and the dishes sparkled. While I worked at drying each dish and glass, I remembered being a teen. When I was fifteen, my dad took me to get my learner's permit. I stood with my birth certificate in hand, turned to my dad behind me in line, and asked about being born so far away. I was told that my mom had gone into labor while they were on their way to California for vacation. It was sort of skimmed over and I never did get all the details. Now, as I thought about it all, it sounded crazy. My mother would have been nine months pregnant, so what was the likelihood they'd be going on a trip to California, just a week before Christmas?

Now today, my mother tells me the hospital was chosen because it was the closest, cleanest facility to the White Mountains? It wasn't hard to figure out that she was keeping a secret. Either that or she was lying and could no longer keep her stories straight.

After the last spoon was dried and returned to its drawer, I put down the towel and sat in a kitchen chair. There was no dealing with this, no resolution, and definitely no getting over it by trying to wash it away. I had to call the one person in my life who I knew would say the right thing.

I called my husband. "Mike, there is something going on.

Mother told me all about Bob's birth and then got almost agitated talking about mine. She kept retreating back to parts of Bob's story. When I pressed her and asked specific questions, she seemed mad. 'You were born in Tucson, that's how it worked out and we're not going to talk about it,' she said in a huff and went to her room. I guess she's in there for the night."

Mike remembered, "Right, the story was they were on their way to California when you were born. Yeah… they were going on vacation. That's why you were born in Tucson."

"So I thought too, but wait. Now the story has changed. It was their choosing to have me in Tucson, since it was the cleanest nearest hospital. Think about it, from the White Mountains to Tucson was closer than driving to Phoenix? I don't think so. I think she protests too much. And why did she change the story?" I wondered.

"So what are you saying? That you may be adopted?"

My thought exactly, and he'd said it out loud. "Yeah…I wonder if I really was adopted? I haven't thought about it for a long time now, but with her stories of Bob and then nothing about me, I am thinking about it again. She actually said, 'and then you popped up.' It was awkward and I could feel that she wasn't telling the truth."

"Let me just look online real quick and see what I can find." His voice trailed as he typed.

"I'm not sure what you're looking for, but I know she's lying or hiding something. I can't believe at this point in time, the end of her life, that she is behaving this way…to me."

I sat in my mother's kitchen frustrated. Speaking the words made it real, even though I didn't want to deal with it.

Mike eagerly shared his idea, "I think we need to do a DNA test. I found a company in California that has a great Web site with instructions, and we can FedEx the samples tomorrow. All you need is a few of your mom's hairs with follicles and a swab of your cheek. Just go through her hairbrush, hold the hair up to the light, and look for little roots. You need about five hairs and all you do is wrap them in a tissue and then put it in an envelope.

Then for your swab, you take two Q-tips and swipe the inside of
your cheek, and then snip the ends off and let them fall into an
envelope. I'll get the FedEx envelope and fill out the forms and
tomorrow we'll put it all together and send it off. It's ninety-nine
dollars, and it takes about three weeks. And then we'll know."

"Wow, okay...cool," I agreed.

We chatted a bit more and he shared what was happening
around our house. I felt connected again and at peace. This was
a great idea.

I hung up the phone and went to work collecting everything.
It helped knowing that Mike would be coming up the next day
and that he was on my side. He was my partner on this quest for
truth. It felt good to do something, so I could stop wondering and
move on.

The topic of my birth had often been a challenge for me.
Mike and I had tossed around the possibility of me being adopted
a few times before, but I always ended up feeling like an ungrate-
ful brat.

When I was younger and asked my mother if I was adopted,
she never answered the question directly. She'd say, "You are
rude. How could you ask me that?" Then she'd carry on about
something she'd recently done for me or bought me. I was made
to feel disrespectful, so much so that even now I felt uneasy. And
I didn't really know why.

It seemed like *our book* was a great idea to help us both cope
with Mother's cancer, but now it also became a chance for me to
confirm or disprove a notion I had felt quietly rambling around in
my head on and off for years. *Was I adopted?*

The notion sent me spinning, but it was so out of this world
that I figured I had to at least hold it together in this solar system
until I knew the truth.

I mused, *I can't have gotten to forty-three without knowing if I
was adopted. Besides, someone would have told me. Right?*

CHAPTER 5

Beginnings and Endings

"When we are no longer able to change a situation, we are challenged to change ourselves."
                                                    —*Victor Frankl*

To LEARN, TO UNDERSTAND, AND TO GROW, one needs information. I needed to get a test comparing my mother's DNA to mine so that once and for all I would know if I was adopted. Whether I was or not, the truth needed to be out in the open.

I've heard so often that family members can all be very different, and siblings can have totally different likes and dislikes. There were differences in my family also, but more than anything I didn't feel like I fit with them. Only when I was young and I was with my grandmother did it feel right. I didn't look completely different from my family, but there wasn't anything that was the same. No one had my ears or nose, my body shape, or even similar hands or feet. No one had asthma, and birthmarks didn't exist. My brother carried features of both my parents, but I never displayed one thing like any of them. They're all early risers while I'm a night owl. They all love barbeque and red meat, and I prefer vegetables. As I got older the differences became more apparent. Vacations, hobbies, and passions were black-and-white different. I shared the same eye color as my mother; however, the way we viewed the world was quite opposite.

In three to four weeks, an email would confirm whether the samples were biological matches—mother to daughter—or not.

It was easy to put it out of my mind and move on, as there was nothing else I could do but wait. I didn't tell my brother or anyone. *I bet I'm adopted...the clues are all in front of me,* I thought while sealing up the FedEx mailer. *We'll just wait and see.*

Each day, Mother and I continued with *our book* and I was in awe of her life and her loving relationship with her parents. I avoided any topic having to do with my childhood and let Mother talk about whatever she wanted.

The following week was about the same with visits and a bit more writing in *our book*. I know that Mother deeply enjoyed all the attention. My brother and I both visited several times a week, spouses in tow, and our kids (her grandchildren) stopped by on many occasions. My daughter Ashleigh spent the night a few times, and my son Hayden and his girlfriend, Jen, made a couple of day trips. Rounding out the family, both of Bob's sons, Dustin and Daniel, and their wives, Julie and Heidi, visited. Mother was thrilled to see all her grandkids and didn't seem upset when asking if there was anything of hers they wanted. It seemed that preparing for the end was not as bad as she had once thought, and she enjoyed hearing which of her prized possessions they loved most.

Although the diagnosis was devastating, Mother loved the time with her family and with Cathy, her best friend. Mother used to work with her, and the entire family appreciated this great friend. Cathy had just moved back to Arizona from Pennsylvania with her husband, Duwayne. She was happy to help and pleased that she could be there for her dear friend. And when we weren't visiting, Cathy was there at least three times a day. She helped Mother with small chores, did shopping for her, and even wrote letters explaining her illness to a few friends down in Phoenix.

Mother loved to write long letters and keep in touch with everyone, especially with her long-time childhood friend from Illinois, Jean. It was painful, but Mother was now unable to write without assistance. There were many phone calls from family in Wales, whom she held close to her heart. Yes, she was dying, but the love, friendship, and concern from everyone around filled her with joy, and this seemed to keep the cancer at bay.

All her life, Mother had been an independent woman. There was never a task, job, or chore that she didn't take care of herself. As she aged, it drove Bob and me crazy to see her up on a ladder painting the ceiling, or with large pruning sheers trimming a tree. We worried that she was doing too much and told her that she needed to ask for help. However, our concern never seemed to sink in, and although there were many scrapes and bruises, Mother's pride in a job well done outweighed any risk.

We feared her independent streak. Could she accept that she'd be even more tired, and that she needed to live more carefully now?

"Mother, you have to take it easy. That is your only job," Bob told her.

"Oh, I know, I'll do it, I'm taking it easy. Besides, Cathy won't let me lift a finger. Did you know she did my dishes the other day?"

"Well that's good; you let her do whatever she wants."

But on the days she did feel pretty good she'd forget about safety. She was alone one day, between Cathy's visits, and went outside to water some plants. Mother loved having plants all around, both inside and out, and every year, as part of her migration up north, most of the plants made the journey too. Outside she had tomato plants, pepper plants, ivy, and several large spider plants. She tended to them regularly, clipping and pruning the leaves and offshoots. These were easy chores for her and she usually performed them in the early-morning hours, which was her favorite time of the day. She had just given them each a nice drink and bent over to move one plant. As she stood up, she lost her balance, fell down hard on her rear end, and then toppled over backward, whacking her head on the ground. Cathy found her an hour later, after she had managed to get back inside. She begged Cathy to keep the accident a secret.

"Honestly Cathy, I'm fine! I only bumped my head and bruised my ego."

Thankfully, Cathy truly was her best friend and called me the same day. "Sue, she just doesn't seem right. For some reason I notice your mom is slower and I don't think it's a good idea for her to be alone. Her fall really has me concerned that it may happen again. You know how stubborn your mom is?"

"You're right, Cathy. It's a safety issue now and she needs to come home. Thank you so much for calling."

I had a long discussion with Bob and we both agreed that it was time for Mother to come down to the valley. We needed to be with her twenty-four/seven and keep her safe from falls.

I called Mother the next morning on my way up north, saying that I wanted to spend some more time with her and I would be there shortly.

She didn't come out to open the gate, didn't even come to the door. Mother was really losing steam now. As I walked in, I stared at the sobering scene in front of me. She sat quietly on the couch, slowly stroking her dog Petey, who lay next to her. Her favorite old girl, DeeDee, lay right in front of her with her head by my mother's feet. It was so quiet. I felt nauseous as I slowly walked in.

"Hi, Mother, are you doing okay?" I spoke softly, fighting back tears.

"There you are," she answered without even looking my way.

"Mom, now don't be mad at Cathy, but she called and told me that you fell. I want you to tell me what happened. We need to make sure you're okay."

"Oh, I'm okay. I'm just a big fool," she said stiffly. "I was outside and didn't pick up these big clunky feet of mine," she explained, moving her feet side to side.

I sat next to her and Petey, and she brightened up a bit.

"So tell me, what happened?" I asked.

"I watered a few plants and my spider plant needed to be out of the sun, so I dropped the hose and picked up the plant and turned to walk. Suddenly I felt a bit dizzy and off-balance, and down I went, right on my butt, and then hit my head." She rubbed a spot towards the back of her head, flinching when she touched the tender area. "It was idiotic, but I'm fine, nothing broken—well except for a pot and a plant."

As we spent the rest of the day together, I noticed she was not the same. She seemed off-balance, her body even wobbly on first standing. The next day was quiet. She slept in, and that was not something Mother did. She also didn't want to eat much. This all concerned me.

While she took a second nap on the same day, I called her doctor. He was saddened by the news.

"Susan, the fall most likely dislodged the cancer, or at least one large tumor. You'll probably see decreased energy and appetite, and probably some pain. Somewhat similar to the way she was feeling it before in her lower back but more widespread. Did I order pain meds for your mom already?"

"Yes, you did, and I have them handy. I think I know the answer to this question, but can you tell me if this means that my mom has less time now?" My voice cracked.

Dr. Gary advised me what to watch for, and how frequently to give Mother her pain meds. Then he calmly answered my question. I did not want to hear this, but it was inevitable.

"Kiddo, you probably have thirty days or less with your mom. I am so sorry."

Bob and I decided that we needed her home, and obviously, she could no longer stay up north in her cabin. In Phoenix, she would be safer and we could take turns staying with her.

When we presented this to Mother, she solemnly agreed. At her request, we planned the move for the following weekend since she was still somewhat stable and had no pain. This gave her a bit more time in the place she loved and a few more days with her close friend, Cathy.

My brother and I, along with our spouses, brought Mother back to the valley with all her personal things. This of course included her two beloved canine companions, DeeDee and Petey. She rode in my car and slept most of the way home. She seemed sad and not very talkative. I'm sure she was also exhausted from the physical preparations, and emotionally drained from having to leave her cabin, permanently.

So, we settled in her Phoenix house. With all of us helping, we were unpacked and eating dinner in no time. When we'd ask about pain, she just answered that she was "okay" or "fine"; but we could see she wasn't. The expression on her face spoke volumes.

Each day following she wanted to eat less and sleep more.

While trying to hold a teacup and raising it up to her mouth, Mother's hand shook and trembled. "Bugger," she'd say and get both hands around it. This lack of strength, and the inability to get up or to hold things was very frustrating for her.

Her once-vibrant voice was now weak and strained, and although she was always happy to see a family member, she didn't tell stories anymore or flash her wide smile. All the simple things became difficult if not impossible for her to do. Mother's spirit was fading.

At night as I'd help her to bed, she would get settled, let out a big sigh, and then hold my hand. I was always up close and near to her in case she wanted to tell me something. I was so hoping she wanted to tell me something. We were face to face, where I could feel her breath faint on my cheek. The next four nights we had our routine.

"Mom, I'm sleeping in the room right next to you if you need anything," I said.

"And you will come," she said softly.

"If you need anything," I finished. "I love you, Mom."

She looked in my eyes and most often didn't say a word. I knew the end was near, and felt she knew it too. It was difficult and painful to watch my mother fade away. The many years she'd lived on this earth did not make it any easier.

That fourth night I called my husband to check in and catch up on the day's events.

"Sue, you got an email from the lab!"

My stomach filled with butterflies. I'd mostly forgotten about the DNA test. I gripped the receiver tight and exhaled. "Read it to me, Mike. Tell me what it says."

"'Glenys is excluded as the biological mother of Susan,'" he read. "No alleles in common...finding was confirmed...second independent analysis..."

"What?" I had heard only parts of it. I couldn't take it all in. "Did you say my mother is excluded as my biological mother?"

Mike read, "With one hundred percent certainty, the providers of both samples are not related."

"Ah...I knew it. I guess I've always known it." But it felt different now—the test made it real. This was something I had never experienced before, some frustration but a bit of victory, too. Almost like figuring out whodunit midway through a mystery.

"Oh Hon, are you okay? How does that make you feel?"

"Mother and I have always been so different, and I hated the differences. I wanted to be the high energy neat-freak career woman who got up each morning at five. I really tried to like camping and fishing and sports. Oh my gosh, she loved watching football. But no, I've been the foster parent, the volunteer with rose-colored glasses, wanting to save society's cast-off children. And take me to a play or a musical and get rid of football. You know?"

"Yeah, so true. But why would your mom keep that from you, Sue? Especially after all the years we did foster care. Wouldn't that have been the perfect time for her to tell you?"

I was really feeling sick. "She never wanted me to know. And I can't say anything to her now. How on earth could I tell her I did a DNA test without her permission?"

While Mother slept, Mike and I talked for hours. As it sank in, I realized how this new truth would affect so many things, in my mind anyway. All I'd known and bonded with regarding my Welsh heritage was gone. My adoptive mother was Welsh, but who was my biological mother? And who was my father? Where were *they* from? And who knew that I was adopted? Bob was almost six when I was born. Surely, he had to know, but he would have told me at some point, wouldn't he? After we hung up, I sat in bed and stewed over the revelation. So many thoughts and questions raced through my mind, and I heard over and over again—*Glenys is excluded as the biological mother of Susan.*

And then it came to me.

I recalled Mother's words from years ago when I shared with her the possibility that Mike and I might adopt one of our foster children. My heart sank as I remembered her response.

Casually, over the phone, she advised me, "Oh no, I don't think you should adopt. You have two of your own that you gave birth to, and you won't love an adopted child the same."

Of course at the time, I thought *Shame on you, Mother. That's ridiculous!*

But now, many years later, I realized I was the adopted child that she didn't love as much as she loved her biological child. I felt a heavy sadness and disappointment for her sharing that despicable opinion with me. Granted, she never intended that I learn I was adopted, or she wouldn't have said that. I know she loved me, but it was different from how she loved Bob. However, this was yet another puzzle piece fitting into its proper place. I lay down on the bed, knees to my chest as I "fit" where I belonged.

Sleep was impossible, so I decided to write my brother a letter, explaining everything. It was perfect timing. Bob was coming the next day to stay the night with Mother, so I could go out to eat with Mike and celebrate our twenty-fifth wedding anniversary. Surely a letter was the best, most discreet way to share this information. Mother wouldn't hear a thing. After all, she had never wanted me to know.

Lying in bed in those early hours of the morning, I wrote these words:

Dear Bob,
This is so hard for me. This has to be the strangest letter I've ever written and I'm sure the most bizarre one you'll ever read. I'll just explain from the beginning about what I've learned, and we'll go from there.

Okay, here goes.... You know Mother and I have been writing her story and going over every detail that she can recall in her life. Well, she was so cute and animated when she said how she learned she was pregnant with you and told many stories about you as an infant and how much she loved you. This of course made me excited to hear about my beginning and learn what I was like as an infant. I couldn't wait to write down the details. However, time and time again Mother avoided this particular story, my story. One time she actually retold parts of your story and I thought she seemed confused, maybe overtired. Finally, I came right out and asked her to tell me about ME.

Mother told me, "Oh Sue, I've been so lucky. To think I would never have children and then to have my Bobby. Oh boy, he was such a joy. I have been so fortunate to have you two kids. I had him and then you popped up—I am a lucky woman."

I was blown away! Then "I popped up"? Really, that is the entire story, and she's done now? Bob, I'm sure you can see how weird that was for me.

I talked to Mike that night and I know I've never seriously talked with you about this, but I have often wondered if I could be adopted. Mike looked online and we ordered a DNA test. I took Mother's hair from her brush, swabbed my cheek, and sent off the samples to a lab.

Well, the results came in today. I know you're going to be shocked, but it says that Mother and I are not biologically related.

Can you believe it? I've wondered on and off for years and after all this time, she never told me or told you.

I want you to know that this doesn't change anything for me. She's my mom and you're my brother, forever.

Anyway, I wanted to let you know. I don't plan on saying anything to Mother about this. I think it would be very upsetting to her and besides, she never planned to tell me and I know those are her wishes.

I love you, MY brother,
Sue

Mike and I agreed to put it aside for the night of our anniversary, which only meant we ignored the elephant in the room. Of course, who I really was and where I came from was all I could think about, anniversary or not.

After spending the night away for the quietest anniversary dinner ever, I returned to Mother's and for a moment considered bringing it up. I planned to play it by ear. If the time was right, maybe I would say something. My mind shifted back and forth, trying to decide what to do.

Sadly, Mother was now barely speaking; mostly only managing to convey *yes* or *no*. She told me with her eyes how happy she was to see me, and I sat next to her holding her hand. I knew at that moment I had to allow her some dignity. I would respect and accept her decision to keep the secret.

As I sat with her, I thought about searching for my birth family and wondered what they would be like. *Maybe they did something with foster children or ran a group home. Maybe I look like them, and maybe I have a big family.* However, today was all about the family I had in my hand—my mother who wanted me by her side.

Holding *our book*, I talked to her about the last topic, her dogs. We had decided they needed their own chapter. I reminded her of all the dogs she'd had in her life and how she and I both love our canine companions.

"Remember your two friends here," I said as I petted Petey and DeeDee. "I promise you that I'll take care of them and they'll fit right in at my house."

She looked at me, and with a slight grin, Mother put her hand on the book. "Okay, it's over," she muttered.

I took that to mean that not only was she done for the moment but probably done forever with all the stories. We were miles away from the joy of *our book*, but because it had been such an important gift on many days, I shared my dreams of the book with her. I put the book down, held both of her hands, leaned in close and spoke softly. "Mother, one day I will write about your life. You're an amazing woman and so special to me, and I want the world to know you."

With a small smile and a strong gaze into my eyes, she listened. "And Mother, you know most likely it will start out with your famous La la La la song and dance. I love that and will never forget it."

A tear trickled down her cheek and she swallowed hard.

"Oh…so many happy times, and I have wonderful memories. I love you and will love you forever and ever," I whispered. Fighting back my tears, I kissed her on the cheek.

She turned her head and I rested her hands gently on the sheet as she fell asleep. I realized then how much my mother really needed me, specifically me, her daughter, adopted or not. It was simple, I was in the right place day after day with my mother, and nothing else mattered. The question of who gave birth to me was gone, for now.

The next day Mother slept a lot, but in the afternoon, she woke up startled, with tears in her eyes. I went over to her and asked if she was okay.

"Mother, I'm right here." I held her hand and made eye contact. "Are you okay?"

"Oh, she's lovely. She's right there," Mother whispered and looked over to the coffee table. She pointed briefly at a card that was propped up.

"Who's there, who do you see?"

"She's not there now, but she was. It was my mom." Ever so slowly she got the words out to tell me what she had experienced. "She was just lovely. She looked beautiful and she was smiling at me."

"That's wonderful, did you talk to her?"

"No, I didn't, but I thought about how much I miss her."

"Oh that's lovely, Mother. Next time you see her, try and talk to her. Tell her that you miss her, okay?"

As she started to fall back asleep she said, "I will. I'll talk to Mom."

Hospice of the Valley had nurses visiting us, helping us to care for Mother at home. They mentioned to me that often their patients see loved ones who have passed, such as a spouse or a parent. Mother's nurse said this is how the dying are provided comfort, perhaps by their deceased loved ones or by God. They seem to feel love, and it often removes fear. Hospice's recommendation was to embrace and encourage this communication with loved ones.

Three days later as she slept, I held Mother's hand for the last time. Her breathing slowed, as she peacefully slipped away.

As tears streamed down my face, I thought, *Mother, I hope you're seeing her. I hope your mom and dad are with you now.*

It was quiet, peaceful, and ever so still. But the serene moment was heavy on my chest—my mother had gone. I felt paralyzed. The silence was deafening. Her raspy breathing had simply stopped and I was in shock. So much had happened in the previous days—the monitoring with Hospice of the Valley, planning the "tag team" care with my brother—and suddenly it was all over.

The concern to do our best, physically and spiritually, was now past. I sat briefly with her small frail shell, holding her cool hand. I was alone and she was really gone.

"God, may you hold my mother dear until I can be with her again," I whispered. I let go of her hand for the final time. The ocean of sadness swelled all around me.

My husband sat with me and said a final prayer. It was just the two of us—I could spiritually feel that she was not on this earth.

The rest of the family gathered at Mother's that night, all of us in shock that the head of our family had passed away. No one knew what to do or what to say. We were just there for Mother, one last time.

As the reality of being without parents sunk in, I was a child again, alone in the world. But this time I was an orphan who was deeply sad. My mother was gone, my father had gone a long time ago, and now I knew they had been my adoptive parents, which meant that my birth mother and father had given me away. I had never once thought of my birth mother in those final days, not until the pain of loss became too unbearable. Susan, the child, needed to find her birth family, because children are precious. Surely, my birth mom wanted to know me. Maybe she was even waiting for me, right?

I was interested in the possibility of these people I belonged to, but for now *my* family was right in front me. My brother and his wife, Mike, our kids.... We had just lost Mother, and I knew there was a lot to do.

CHAPTER 6

Crossroads

"Sometimes we stare so long at a door that is closing we see too late the one that is open."
—Alexander Graham Bell

"BEES—I HAVE BEES BUZZING AROUND inside my head," I told Mike. We sat at the table having breakfast on our first day home after my mother's death. The next day we'd meet Bob and his wife, Rosanna, to begin the task of going through Mother's things.

Mike glanced at me, concerned. "What do you mean about bees?"

"I can't believe my mother is gone. Just a short time ago, I talked to her every day, and spent every Wednesday with her. I shared every little thing, every secret, the good, the bad, and the ugly. Suddenly there's this hole in my life—she's missing. At the same time, I feel really mad. I'm angry with her for keeping such a big secret."

It wasn't about loss or the job ahead, but so many memories were flooding my brain that I felt frazzled and confused. Each small piece of her buzzed and hummed and flung itself around inside my mind. It was utterly chaotic, like jigsaw pieces raining down—some falling into place in my newly found adoption puzzle, but some completely missing the table and scattering on the floor. I felt excited, nervous, and overwhelmingly sad, all at the same time.

Looking back, I can see how the "bees" were a positive thing.

All that buzzing activity allowed me to hold it together and keep my sanity. I felt the loss of my mother to some degree, but it was such a confusing time. This disorientation helped me keep my head above water in the deep, dark well of grief... at least for a little while.

Later that day, my husband and I moved things around in the garage, knowing that soon I'd have many of my mother's items to bring home. We condensed our kids' old boxes and decided to toss old shoes and clothes. While looking through a box marked "Sue/Ash—purses & hats," I found an envelope sticking out of an old purse. It was from a visit with an astrologer over ten years earlier, and inside I found all my notes and my astrological chart. Honestly, at that moment the idea of a fun mental break was appealing, so I pulled up a chair and started reading.

The heading at the top of the first page read:

Genesis, Chapter 1—verse 14, And God said let there be lights in the firmament of the heaven to divide the day from the night; and let them be for signs, and for seasons, and for days, and years.

At the bottom was information about understanding astrology and natal horoscopes, along with the astrologer's name, Erica, and her phone number.

I'd taken notes based on Erica's reading of my chart, and listed details that she provided to me.

Reading over my headings and notes, I became intrigued by her thoughts, questions, and predictions. I remembered my visit and the hour-long discussion with her. This had been over a decade ago, but it felt as if I'd just beem there. I sat in the moment, reading and remembering.

Erica, the astrologer, did business out of her home. She was the weekly guest on a popular morning radio show, which is how I found her. However, I felt a little apprehensive about my reading. Several co-workers and I thought it would be fun to see what she had to say, but I didn't take it too seriously.

Erica's home was beautiful, in a very upscale area with a magnificent entryway. *Well, at least she's successful,* I thought as I rang the doorbell.

The door opened. "Hi, I'm Erica, and you must be Susan," she said, extending her hand.

We shook hands. "It's great to meet you, Erica. I've been looking forward to this afternoon—I waited three weeks for an appointment."

"Great, me too. Come on in and let's get started." Erica had long blonde hair and a warm smile. She guided me to her home office and we sat down at a beautiful oak desk.

As she looked over her prepared information, she confirmed my date and time of birth. "Okay, you were born at two-eleven in the afternoon on December eighteenth, a week before Christmas. Wow, what a present you were, right?"

"Yes, my mother always tried to keep my birthday and Christmas separate. The day after my birthday, we'd put up the Christmas tree and decorate. It worked well—a shorter season with the house in disarray."

Erica let me know that we would go over some things and that if I had specific questions I could ask them towards the end. I thought that was perfect, because I didn't have any questions at that point.

"First thing," she said, looking at me with surprise. "Something big happened when you were born."

"Hmm… no, not that I know of. I was small, my mom once told me. But I've never heard that there was any problem."

"Maybe *around* your birth, say within the first three months, something life-changing, altering, happened *to you*. Does that sound like anything you would have heard about from your mom or dad?"

"Wow, not at all, but I'll ask and see what I can come up with." I wrote on my pad of paper: *Something happened TO me when I was born—within the first three months!*

"Let's talk about more recent events. You married when you were young, right? You have kids and you take care of kids?"

"I did, I got married at eighteen and we have two kids."

"And there are other children in your life, or you take care of them?"

"We did foster care for a few years, but it was hard on my kids so we stopped," I explained. "My kids were just four and six years old at the time and they were learning some things that were not appropriate. We fostered a sibling group of three, between the ages of two and five years old, for about a year. As soon as they were placed with a family we didn't take any more foster children."

"Which explains to me what I'm seeing for you down the road, that you will have *more* kids in your life." She nodded to herself as she studied my chart.

I fidgeted in my chair and told her, "Oh, no way, my husband didn't really enjoy the experience. I don't think we'll be doing it again. It was something I really wanted to do, but foster care involves the entire family, a twenty-four/seven way of life. And he had a vasectomy, which takes care of any more natural-born children."

"Well, you'll have to let me know… say, within the next five years how things work out." Erica leaned forward and looked at me intently. "Now let's talk about your kids. I see a monumental change in your life and it's coming from your daughter when she's around eighteen. Your kids, they're your life and you love them very much, but you have to remember that a parent's job is to raise their children to be the best adults they can be. Then you have to let them go and spread their wings and be independent. With independence come mistakes, and that's how we all learn. Yes, she'll cause you great trouble and there will be challenges."

"Erica, my daughter Ashleigh is amazing—and right now she's ten. I cannot imagine that she'd cause any real trouble; it's not her nature. She is the kindest, most helpful and caring young lady. Seriously, everyone loves her, and I mean that; even her brother who's eight years old adores her, and they're best friends."

I'm starting to wonder about this astrologer as I write down:

Our family will have more kids, or watch more kids?

Ashleigh will cause us great trouble when she's eighteen.

Erica continued, "Your son, he's basically steady and he'll do very well, be well known, somewhat famous as an adult."

"That does not surprise me—Hayden is very different. Even at eight he has a unique personality and sense of humor. I can totally see him as an actor or maybe even in politics, but Ashleigh and trouble, I cannot see that."

"Let's talk about death, if that's all right?" Erica asked.

I nodded. "I'm a Christian, and death doesn't really freak me out, so that's fine."

"Well, good then." She laughed. "You know that when a body dies it's just a shell, the body we were given for our time here. I don't have information that someone in particular is going to die, and if I did I wouldn't share that. But everyone has death in their family and I wanted to touch on the subject. You've had people in your family die before, and although it can feel like you can't continue on, you do. We all do; we all feel the devastation and loss, but we have the strength inside to move forward."

I write down: *Someone close to me is going to die, I think??*

"Erica, I know you can't tell me who, but my husband's grandmother, GG, is older and has cancer. My mother is pretty healthy, but older. We're close to both of them. GG lives in Iowa, so we don't see her very often. The rest of the family really isn't old, but my niece Lexi has cancer. She's young and going through treatment; we're all really hopeful, but she's only six. Is there anything else you can tell me?"

Erica smiled and said, "Just know that when you lose someone close to you, you carry that person with you. You have to be thankful for the time you had together. Try and find happiness in the moment, and should they pass on in the next two or three years, you'll have peace when it's their time to go."

I printed in all capital letters:

I THINK MY MOM IS GOING TO DIE IN THE NEXT FEW YRS!

We continued talking about many things. The personal struggles in my marriage, jobs I'd had, and general philosophies on finding your life's work. At times, it felt like Erica was dead on, and other times, it was like she was hinting at something but it didn't pertain to me. It was uncanny how she knew things about my life that had already happened. Historically, I was hard pressed to find one thing wrong in her reading.

All in all, I remembered the session as being intriguing as I sat looking at the notes from that day. Then I sat straight up with a jolt—all those years ago, Erica knew I was adopted! That had to be what she saw. *My birth mother put me up for adoption after I was born.* My skin was tingling, my heart was racing, it was as if I had been Tased by the adoption universe.

So, that was the life-changing event! "Holy crap, she was trying to tell me that within three months of my birth, I was put up for adoption," I said out loud. My voice echoed in the quiet garage.

And the other notes? Once I thought about them, they were just as accurate. Well, except for the one about my mother dying in the next two to three years. It was more like ten years.

I wondered, *maybe someone else, maybe my birth mom had passed away in that time frame.*

However, back then Lexi did pass away when she was seven and then the next year GG died. And Erica was right about foster care, we got our license again and had ten wonderful children enrich our lives. Ashleigh causing trouble at age eighteen was an understatement, and I can see Hayden being famous as he's in his fourth year of film school.

But most important to me, as I sat holding the notes from ten years ago, was the fact that I had indeed been adopted. It was part of me and even though my beginning was kept a secret, it didn't change the truth. When I came into this world, my birth mother gave me away. It was as if God had stuck me with this invisible cosmic label: *ADOPTED.* I was born to a woman and man who didn't want me, and I was given to parents who wanted a baby. Erica could see the label since the universe didn't care that my adoptive parents wanted it to be kept secret.

It made me wonder—*how did she know?* I wished *I* had known. And why couldn't my mother tell me, after all the years we'd had together? After all the things we'd done alone together… why not tell me?

There I was, at a crossroads. One path led to my mother, my loss, my grief and feelings of betrayal, but also *our book*. The other path led to a bright white, empty space with a door at the center. It was nothing but the unknown. And with so much sadness surrounding my mother's death and knowing that she had kept this huge secret from me, it was easy to choose the path to the door, to see what and whom I might find.

CHAPTER 7

Confidential Intermediary

"Great difficulties may be surmounted by
patience and perseverance."
> — *Abigail Adams*

I QUICKLY LEARNED that the laws in Arizona protect the privacy of both the birth mother and the adoptive parents. However, they completely ignore the primary person in the adoption triad, the child. Adoptees have no rights to their birth information and cannot even get their own original birth certificate. It's all sealed, and I was denied access.

All I had to go on was a DNA test and my altered birth certificate. I joined online groups and participated in the discussion areas, always requesting advice and help. My odd little certificate didn't even say which hospital I was born in; only that it was Tucson, Arizona. In pencil on the back, someone had written my size and weight.

I registered with International Soundex Reunion Registry (ISRR) and Adoptees' Liberty Movement Association(ALMA). I also joined the American Adoption Congress and LateDiscovery.org. Who knew there was a group for people whose birth stories had been kept from them, just like me? Locally, a new friend encouraged me to attend a support group called Search Triad. I was full of hope for finding my birth family, as many had done before me.

Not long into the process, and after many brick walls, it was suggested that I look into hiring a Confidential Intermediary (CI) to continue my search. Another option was to ask the state for my non-identifying information and hope for details that would help me to search on my own. My heart needed to find my birth mother as soon as possible, so I chose the CI route. Not all states allow CIs, but Arizona does use the program. The end goal is to reunite families who were separated by adoption. I researched and found that CIs are appointed by the Arizona Supreme Court. Remarkably, they have access to everything—court documents, adoption decrees, even the original birth certificate. However, their job is solely to make contact. They inform birth families that a family member is looking for them, get the appropriate releases signed and notarized, and only then provide the contact information to the person searching. A CI does not share information they may find along the way. The information is used for searching and then contacting, that is all.

I read about the program on the Arizona Supreme Court's Web site. It seemed that a CI would be able to cut through everything and lead me to what I wanted. I searched the Internet and found someone not far from me. Her Web site seemed good enough and the price reasonable, so I hired her. I downloaded forms, filled them out, had them notarized, and dropped all necessary items in an envelope.

Simple, right?

After I mailed my info to the CI who had a local P.O. Box, I continued to participate in message boards and attend Search Triad support meetings. I learned that maybe I'd been too swift, that I should have interviewed a few CIs before hiring. All CIs are not created equal, apparently, and it wasn't long before I learned that lesson the hard way. In my haste, I'd hired the great Arizona Confidential Intermediary Nazi. She was an adoptee herself, and was in reunion with her father, so I thought she'd certainly be sensitive to my cause, but I was wrong. Her MO was to follow the rules and even go beyond the letter of the law. When in doubt, she over-documented and seemed to take every opportunity to slap me in the face with her interpretation of the rules. She was not only insensitive, she was rude, and I soon knew I had chosen the wrong intermediary.

After a couple of weeks, my CI told me that she'd received a copy of my original birth certificate which directed her search to another city. Naturally, I was filled with questions.

"You're looking at my original birth certificate? Where it lists my real mother and father's names, the hospital I was born in and my height/weight? *You have that?*"

This was fantastic. She actually had a copy of this elusive, super-secret document.

"So what hospital was I born in? What did my birth mother name me?"

"I cannot give you any information," she droned. "The rules governing Confidential Intermediaries are blah blah blah...."

"Well, why do you have to go to another city? What city?" I asked.

"You were born in Tucson and after making a phone call, I learned your adoption took place in Tucson. You said you were adopted in Phoenix, but that is not true."

I didn't want to argue and didn't even understand what her issue was, but I became very direct. I lowered my voice and slowed it way down. "Barbara, I told you my adoptive parents lived in the White Mountains, but that they had moved to Phoenix, so most likely I was adopted in Phoenix. I don't care what city I was adopted in, search where you need to search."

"Yes, I'm going to write for the adoption agency paperwork and that should lead to your birth mother. Good bye." *Bam* — the phone cracked in my ear as it was slammed down.

Yes, I understand privacy rules, but it's an odd feeling when your personal history is basically off-limits to you. Shouldn't just knowing that all this was recent news to me have given Barbara understanding for my plight and increased her sensitivity? It appears not. Not only was she rude, she seemed irritated that I didn't know *where* I was adopted. I was over-the-top frustrated that this woman had my birth certificate copy in her hand and was not allowed to give it to me or tell me what it said. Did my birth mother name me? Was my birth father listed? All questions I couldn't know the answers to in a document about my birth that I couldn't see, much less have. Ever. I was even more offended by the fact that she hung up on me.

After our brief conversation, and after venting to my husband, life went on as usual. Mike and I went to an afternoon movie for a well-needed mental break. In the following days we found things to enjoy and entertain us while we waited. He had work and I had a lot of housework to catch up on.

An email came about a week later stating that Barbara had read my file at the adoption agency and had some good information to help with the search.

"Read my file? There's a file about me? What was the reason for giving me up? How old was my birth mom? How old was my birth father, and were they together?" I wondered out loud, talking to the computer monitor.

Faced with complete ignorance about my own beginnings, my mind tried to fill in the gaps. The only thing I knew for sure was that I wasn't like my adoptive family at all. We were different in so many ways. For example, as I got older I found myself drawn to children and volunteering. As a teen, I knew I wanted to do foster care at some point. My mother rolled her eyes at me, dismissing my lofty plan. I assumed she didn't even understand what foster care was. Now, I was grateful to have a better understanding of why I was so different. But not far from those thoughts lived the notion that somewhere was a family who was more like me, and I couldn't wait to get to them.

Hungering for information, I required my CI to abide by her timeline. When a date passed with no word, I was on the phone calling for an update. The Court system allows CIs to charge an hourly fee, a fee for paperwork and processing, and a direct fee for any expenses they incur, such as photocopies or gas for travel. My CI insisted on an initial retainer fee, which would more than likely cover all the required fees, or so she said. But it wasn't long before she'd gone through the entire retainer and needed another deposit to continue her work. After receiving an itemization for the expenses, I mailed off another check. I got my update, and Barbara kept working after she received my second check.

One day she called when I was out and left me a message. The voice mail said, "I'm having trouble finding your birth mother because her date of birth is not listed anywhere. In the adoption paperwork her age was given, but no specific date of birth. I do have a few ideas and I should know more in a couple of days."

I was traumatized by my forced position in this transaction — *sit there and take it.* Each time I would talk with Barbara or receive an email or message, I couldn't ask anything. I had no way to verify what she did or didn't work on. I felt as if I were tied to a chair, blindfolded, mouth taped shut, and subjected to a slow torture. It was like a vulture pecking away at my chest, trying to get at my heart. I was depressed, discouraged, and all the while alone on this frightening helpless journey. I had my family, but no one really understood what it felt like to not know where you come from.

I had given birth to two children and I remembered what a miracle it was, and such a joyful time in all of our lives. My family and my husband's family all celebrated both children as they came into the world. That's the norm. But I simply couldn't comprehend what it might be like when a baby is given up for adoption. It seemed to me it must have to be less joyous, probably even mournful. That had been my beginning.

After my CI took a vacation, worked on other cases, and got additional money from me, she finally called with news I could hold on to. She had something to tell me, and it had taken three months.

When I saw her name on the caller ID, I quickly answered, "Hello, this is Susan."

"This is Barbara the CI, is Susan there?"

Oh good God, is she kidding? "Yes, this is Susan."

"Well, Susan, it's been a job tracking her down," Barbara chuckled. "But, I have found your birth mother, and she is deceased...um, for a while now, actually. And your grandparents are deceased as well. That's why it was so hard to find her." More chuckles.

My eyes filled with tears and my heart sank. *What are you laughing at?* I thought. I was blown away and devastated. I had considered this outcome as a possibility, but because my birth mother would be in her early sixties I had dismissed the thought. I deeply needed to meet her, but it wasn't going to happen; in one sentence the hope of meeting my mother was obliterated.

"Oh," was all I could manage to say. I was quiet for a few seconds while trying to process the thought of my birth mother being gone.

"Did you understand me? *Your birth mother is dead.*"

"Yeah, umm…when did she die?" I was fighting hard not to cry on the phone.

"The laws in Arizona prohibit me from telling you any specific information I find, but it does allow me to inform you of your search subject's death. I can tell you that you have half-siblings based on a conversation I had, while confirming your birth mother's death. It would be very easy at this point to search and contact a sibling if you'd like me to do that."

"Oh, I don't know." My voice was shaking. "I guess since it would be easy." I was trembling. "I have to go now, but I'll get back with you." I pushed the end button on the phone, and it felt like the end of me.

In my head, I had assumed it was God's plan for me to find my birth family now, *after* my mother was gone. I could build a relationship with my birth family, as a sort of a second chapter in my life. I had so hoped this new chapter would be filled with family members like me or who at least looked like me. I'd had it worked out spectacularly in my mind, to have this new relationship free from guilt. But now the door was slammed shut on that idea, and I felt the enormous burden of loss all over again. It was difficult to process, and difficult to find peace. And the way the information was delivered caused me great emotional pain.

I wondered, *How long ago had she passed? How old was she?*

Did she ever look for me? Did anyone even know about me? I had so many questions. Now the only way to have even a glimmer of finding answers was to locate my half-sibling.

Mike sat behind me at the dining room table listening to my side of the conversation. When I finally turned around I could see that he understood the basic information Barbara had conveyed.

"I am so sorry, Hon. I'm sitting here in shock." Fighting back tears, he said, "I can't believe your birth mom is gone."

We had both held out "what if" hopes and deeply wanted to meet my first mother. And since that was now off the table we discussed what to do next. At first, I felt as if I was done. I was almost too afraid to keep looking. *What if my half-sister was killed in a car accident with my mother?* I wondered. *Could I bear any more loss?*

The next morning I got an email from the CI, with a subject line that simply read "New case."

I thought, *What? A new case?, She probably has me confused with someone else.* I opened the email and read the message.

Barbara quoted the rules, telling me that I had to fill out all the paperwork again, and things would start as a new search, new retainer and all. To conduct a sibling search, she claimed, still required her to do all the necessary paperwork and inquiries. The email was three pages long, stating all the codes for the CI process as if I were a new client. With the exception of the part added at the end pertaining to a sibling search, I had a form letter.

Only the day before she had notified me of my birth mother's death, and now she simply sent me a form letter.

I typed furiously: *You made it sound like you already have a name—you just have to get a number and then you'll call, not go through all of the paperwork again! Are you serious?"*

Of course, this woman lacking in human compassion and basic common sense *was* serious, and sent me all of the rules, *again!* There's nothing more painful than feeling like you're so close to answers…so close to finding someone in your birth family—yet having serious concerns about being taken advantage of by a CI who's working with no one providing oversight.

After a lot of consideration, and thinking about searching on my own, I concluded that I still had no tangible information. I didn't even know my mother's name or the family's last name.

Fearing that I was too close to the forest, I spoke to my husband and kids. We mulled it over for a couple of days while the paperwork sat on my desk. The pros and cons were carefully considered, and we all came to the same conclusion.

In the words of my daughter, Ashleigh, "The fastest way of getting to family and getting your own information is through the CI, even if she is an asshat." She is plain-spoken.

When people are beyond difficult and painfully annoying, we give them the "asshat" label. My CI, on most occasions, was unprofessional and unsympathetic—not to mention a poor businessperson with horrible grammar who lacked basic email etiquette. Those are the nicest things I can say about her. Yes, Barbara was an asshat.

A few weeks later, I received an email that stated Barbara had found my half-sibling and that she was female. She knew her name and got a phone number from an aunt. This was the aunt who had confirmed that my birth mother was deceased. The CI believed I also had a male half-sibling and wanted to mention that in case I preferred contact with him. I told Barbara to contact the female, as she already knew her name and number.

Two days later the CI called when I was out and left me a message. I retrieved the voice mail and listened:

"Susan, I have called your half-sister at three different times of the day and no one is answering. I will leave a message on the next call if it is not answered. Goodbye."

Oh really? She'll *now* leave a message on the next call. What a good idea! I rolled my eyes. I don't answer the phone if I'm not expecting a call or know who it is. I'll wait for the caller to leave a message, listen to it, and then react accordingly. *I guess in asshatland it works differently and people there answer every phone call.*

Thankfully, the message prompted my half-sister to return her call. She in turn also had to leave a message for Barbara. A few days later they did speak and the CI explained how it was necessary for her to sign and notarize an affidavit allowing the

CI to share her contact information with me. Sadly, my half-sister worked long hours and wasn't able to get the form notarized quickly.

After a few days, an email came explaining the situation. The CI reiterated that as soon as she received the form—properly filled out and notarized—she would call me with my half-sister's information. The email also explained that I had an outstanding balance on my account, and that she wouldn't want to hold up any information for non-payment of expenses.

After all the waiting, after all I'd been through just to get to this point, dealing with loss and devastation, I really did not see blackmail as part of an asshat's repertoire, but I opened the attached PDF statement and saw that it was for $2.54. I was being threatened over less than three dollars.

So I paid the outstanding invoice and put it all behind me—with good documentation to be used another day, along with a formal complaint to the Arizona Supreme Court.

CHAPTER 8

Sisters

---

*"I do not believe that the accident of birth
makes people sisters and brothers. It makes them
siblings. Gives them mutuality of parentage.
Sisterhood and brotherhood are conditions people
have to work at."*

—Maya Angelou

FINALLY, I KNEW MY SISTER'S NAME, and it was Lucy. I had a sister. Such a unique concept to me. A half-sister, but sister nonetheless, and it felt surreal. To think that just a few months prior, my world had been caring for my mother and focusing on the difficulty of losing a loved one. I'd had no idea there was another family living out there in the world with a biological connection to me.

Once I had Lucy's information and phone number, I took a couple of hours to organize my thoughts. Everything I had read in preparation advised me to get a pad of paper and write down specific questions. I readied my notebook, had tissue nearby, my No. 2 pencil, two pens (in case one happened to stop working and my pencil to break), then sat down with the phone in hand.

I started dialing, and about half-way through, I thought, *Uhh, what do I say?*

I stopped, pushed the end button, and hung up. *Oh my gosh, when she answers the phone, what do I say?* "Hi, my name is Susan and I'm your half-sister?"

What if the CI got it wrong, or what if she doesn't know about me and thinks this is some hoax? Maybe I should say my whole name and that I found out I was adopted and hired a CI and she had found *you*, possibly my half-sister.... Hmmm... that might be best. It was the night before Thanksgiving—she might not even be home, or maybe she'd have company. *Oh, I wonder if I have any nieces or nephews.* I went into my husband's office and asked him and my son what they thought.

They smiled at each other and Mike said, "Just call her and start by saying your name. It'll be fine." Hayden turned his head away and down and I sensed that I was being pretty silly.

Mike made it sound so easy, like this call was no big deal. But it was a monumental deal to me. This was it—*she* was it, and there was no one else. If this phone call went badly, my one and only link to my family would be broken. I had to get out of my own head and move past the negative thoughts.

"Okay, I can do this." I sighed. Trying to shake off the nerves, I wriggled and hopped up and down a few times. I went back to the living room to my place all set up on the couch, and picked up the phone again. Anxiety started creeping in again as I yelled to the other room, "Okay, keep quiet, I'm calling."

They laughed. "Okay, you call, we'll be quiet," Mike said.

The phone was ringing. A woman's voice said, "Hello?"

"Hi, my name is Susan, and..."

The voice interrupted, "Oh hi, it's me, Lucy. Can you hang on a second?"

Of course I could! I thought, *Whew...Okay, this is going to be okay, she sounds nice—yay!*

"Okay, I'm back," Lucy said. "Sorry about that, I'm getting things ready for Thanksgiving and just needed to take something out of the oven."

"Oh, right. I'm so sorry to bother you just before a holiday. Do you have a little time to talk?" My voice shook.

"Yeah, I've been waiting for your call. Well, waiting for that woman to finally give you my number; but really, I've been waiting for years. I've always known about you, and thought that one day you'd call one of us."

I sat back on the couch and joy pooled up in my eyes. I asked, "You've always known about me? You were waiting for me?"

I had felt unwanted and my world had gotten so small. The person I thought loved me the most had kept the biggest secret from me—but here was someone telling me she'd been waiting for me. It was overwhelming, and I felt so much hope and excitement for this relationship.

"Lucy, how did you know about me?"

"Oh Susan, I've just always known about you, from as far back as I can remember. I was a child when Kathy told me about the baby she had given up for adoption."

"Kathy? My birth mother's name is Kathy? Oh, I have so many questions. I know she's deceased, the CI told me that, but tell me about her and you and your family."

"Okay, her name, um—our *mother's* name was Kathleen Fay Bardlow. She was sent away to have you when she was about six or seven months along. It was her mother who made all the plans."

At last! I picked up my pencil and started taking notes. First, in large fancy cursive I wrote Kathleen. *My mother who gave life to me was named Kathleen.*

"Her parents were David and Nancy, and she had five siblings: Sharon, Davey, Leslie, Steven, and Denise. David and Nancy, our grandparents, passed away awhile ago, but her brother and sisters are all alive. She had an older brother, two older sisters and then twins, a sister and brother who are eight years younger. Kathy, my mom, *our mom*, passed away in 1999. She was fifty-three."

As she spoke, I took notes swiftly with as much detail as possible. I tried to remove myself from the situation and not think, but just write.

I went into newspaper reporter mode, asking, "What was my mom's date of birth? What date did she pass away, and, if you don't mind telling me, how did she die? Did she have any other kids? Do you know who my birth dad is?"

We talked for almost four hours that night, each switching

phones as they would run out of juice. I tried to learn as much as possible from Lucy, my sister.

I discovered I had a big birth family, and my mother went on to marry and have four more kids, Lucy being the next one born after me. My grandparents each came from big families, and my aunts and uncles have many children. I began to feel I had missed out on an entire life.

In my adoptive family, I grew up with no grandparents on my dad's side. My grandparents on my mother's side passed away when I was thirteen, and my mother was an only child. I did have my brother, but we were seriously lacking in extended family.

I shared this comparison with Lucy, trying to explain my sadness on missing out on this great big family, and how I'd just lost my mother.

"Lucy, I was with Mother when she passed away, and I had just found out that I was, in fact, adopted. I had clues growing up but I never pushed it, and my mother had a story for my beginning and why I was born in Tucson. You know the hardest thing for me has been something that my mother told me a few years ago. When I discussed the possibility of adopting a foster child she told me that I wouldn't love that child the same as my two birth children. My mother continued on to explain how it wasn't fair to the child. He should be adopted by someone who hasn't had their own baby.

"I wasn't concerned about my love for him or if he would feel differently, and I thought my mother's advice was wrong—crazy wrong, actually. We ended up not adopting him for other reasons, but Lucy, the moment I found out I was adopted, those words of my mother's popped right into my head. I thought about how they now pertained to *me*, the adopted child."

"Wow. Well, I can tell you that…" she tried to explain, but I went on to get my point across.

"Lucy, it's been so hard to deal with being adopted. She lied to me *and* didn't love me as much as Bob, but I loved her so much. Especially in the last, say, ten years. But my mother never had enough faith in our relationship to tell me something so important. It means the world to me to find you and learn all about my family."

I needed to know them, I wanted to fit in and be a part of their lives. Even though my birth mother was gone, there was still the remainder of a family, *my* family.

The illusion I was putting together came tumbling down when she told me of her childhood and family.

"Oh, Susan…now listen to me. I need to tell you some things. You were so much better off! Honest, you need to hear that. My grandmother had serious mental health issues and was abusive to everyone. She needed to be on medication, and I don't think she ever was. Each of her children had many challenges and multiple marriages—they're very dysfunctional.

"Kathy married my father, Theo, about a year after you were born. Then I came along, next my sister Jackie, and then my brothers Teddy and Leo. Some time after Teddy was born I became fearful. I didn't understand why my parents fought so much. Teddy, my sister, and I would hide under a blanket together when all the yelling was going on, and young Leo would just cry. Even when my mom was holding him or he was on the floor, he screamed and cried all the time.

"It was around then that I learned about you. I think I was in school, maybe first grade, and Kathy told me that she'd had a baby that her mom made her give away. It was so confusing for me as a child thinking that my *gran* made my mom give her baby to some stranger! I felt so bad for Mom. She was a sad person who cried a lot. Then I learned that most of it was over losing you."

I held my hand over the phone so she couldn't hear me cry. There was so much sadness and loss in all these revelations. They weighed heavily on my chest, pressing my hope down lower and lower.

Lucy went on. "It was just before Christmas one year and I was so excited to put up the tree. Mom was in her room. When I went to get her, I asked if we could finish the decorating. Well, she could hardly talk, and I knew she'd been crying. I'll never forget her answer. She said, 'I'm sorry, I can't stop thinking about my baby. I miss her and I hope she's okay.' It was that way every Christmas—she was missing you and worried about you."

At that moment I realized how difficult it had been for Lucy. Christmas is every child's favorite time of the year, and my mother—our mother—couldn't get over the loss of her firstborn child, even though she'd had four children after.

Lucy continued, "Just so you'll know how hard it was, I want to tell you this, and I don't want you to feel bad or think bad of me. When I was about ten, I told my mom, 'I wish you had given *me* away and I had been adopted.' I was so sick of it. But, there wasn't anything she could do, and she only talked to me about it. She treated me like a friend, a confidante, rather than her daughter."

"I am so sorry, Lucy. It sounds like she never dealt with the loss. But, was she fine the rest of the year?" I asked.

"You came up often. Her relationship with my dad was volatile and they fought all the time. Yes, I have to say, even the rest of the year was horrible. My dad would hit her, and then she'd plot her revenge and attack him when he least expected it. Then the police would come. It was horrible.

"It was one of their fights that led to her trying to commit suicide. I think she did something over the top and we were probably going to be taken away by child services. She just couldn't take it. We were sent off to live with different people—aunts, and my grandparents at one point. All four of us were unstable, frightened, and had no idea what was going on.

"Finally, our parents divorced and we lived with Kathy, but she was not responsible. I think I had just turned eleven. We always had money problems and didn't live in one place very long. I do think she tried her best, but her best wasn't very good, to be honest. She had a lot of boyfriends, and most of the time they would end up abusing her.

"When she was about forty she finally met a nice guy. His name was Marc. They married and she seemed really happy."

I went back to reporter mode, a safer place to learn and get information. "When she passed away, was Marc with her?" I asked.

"No, Marc passed away before she did. He had some health problems and was on state aid, and I'm not exactly sure what happened, but he had seizures and then one day Kathy called and said he had died."

"Oh, that is so sad. She was finally in a happy place and then he died. What did she do after he passed away?" I asked.

"My sister moved in, along with her daughter, and then eventually my brother Teddy moved in as well. It was not a good thing, and it sounded to me like they were taking advantage of her. I think my mother felt guilty for not being a very good parent, so she let them walk all over her. She didn't have much, but what she had she shared with them. My sister and brothers were addicts, and I knew something bad was going to happen. I had to force myself to let go of my mother so I could go on with my life, my family. You know? Sometimes it's all you can do to just take care of yourself."

I totally understood and I was sad. Sad for not finding the family I thought I needed. But at that moment, I was sad for my sister, who had to be in turmoil and reliving it all. "Yes, Lucy, that was the right thing to do. I'm sure your family was better off for it."

"I don't know about that," Lucy said. "I think I've been somewhat dysfunctional as well. We all have, especially my sister and oldest brother.

"One night, my younger sister Jackie called me about four in the morning and said that Kathy had died. Susan, I wasn't surprised. First, she had health problems—a heart condition and diabetes. Yet she smoked and ate junk food. Second, I knew there were drugs being used, so it was just a matter of time. Even though it was expected, Kathy was only fifty-three, and her death, that permanent loss, was very hard. Of course it was me and my husband who took care of everything and made the arrangements."

As I sat with my rounded No. 2 and pages of information, I felt a deep sorrow. I didn't have this great family waiting for me after all. My birth mother was a despondent woman who made poor choices and died at a young age. It was not as I'd hoped, and I was acutely disappointed.

Lucy and I agreed to share pictures and exchanged email addresses, so I focused on that. I had several pictures scanned and waiting in my computer to send. I sent shots of me as a baby, as a child and teen, when I got married, and then a current photo. I still couldn't wait to see what my birth mother looked like and wondered if I looked like her.

Lucy coyly asked, "Do you have blonde hair and blue eyes? Oh, and are you tall?"

"Yeah, how did you know that?" Her question really surprised me.

"Kathy was that way, and I had a feeling." Her voice lowered, almost sounding disappointed. "Well, I just knew it."

"What, is there something wrong?"

"No, but I told my husband that you and I would be like that movie, *Twins*. You're Arnold—tall, blonde and beautiful—and I'm the Danny De Vito character." She chuckled.

"So you're shorter and look different than I do?" I tried not to laugh, but I'm sure she could hear the humor in my voice.

"Oh yeah, my dad was Italian and stocky, so I have dark hair and I'm short, and you're this tall blonde, just like *Twins*, you know?"

"Ah yes, that *is* really funny." I laughed out loud, and on the inside I felt proud that she assumed I was beautiful. Even though we'd had different lives, I felt great kinship with Lucy being able to laugh in the middle of all the darkness.

"Lucy, I can't wait to see the pictures of Kathy and of you. Any pictures you have of family and want to share, I'll so enjoy and love having."

We burned up the Internet late into the night, emailing pictures and comments back and forth. I was astonished at how much alike my birth mother and I looked as kids. It melted my heart to see someone who looked so much like me. Any adoptee will tell you that it's an amazing feeling to see your nose or your eyes on a parent. We usually grow up never seeing anyone who looks like us, until we have children.

As time went on and Christmas neared, I wanted to reach out

to whatever family was left. Lucy gave me her sister's name and address and I wrote to her right away. *If she's anything like Lucy, Jackie and I will hit it off great,* I thought. Also, I asked Lucy to share the addresses of my aunts and uncles, but out of concern for their privacy she didn't feel comfortable giving them to me. However, it was easy for me to find them on my own, once I had names to search for.

So, I sent a special Christmas card to each of them, and enclosed a few pictures and this letter.

December 17, 2008
Dear Aunts and Uncles,
I'm writing to wish you Merry Christmas and explain who I am.

Your sister, Kathy, was my birth mom and I was born on December 18, 1964. I realize we are total strangers and our connection is genetic, but I would love to know more about you, your family, my mother, & my grandparents. Anything you can share would be truly wonderful!

In case you're curious about me: I learned I was adopted about three months ago, at the end of my adoptive mother's life. I often wondered if I was adopted, especially after seeing my birth certificate around the time I learned to drive. I was born in a town about two hours away and my mother changed the reason two or three times as to why I was born in Tucson, so far away. Finally, when she was very ill (this past August) and I was living with her, we decided to write down her life story...to write a book of sorts. Mother was really sad and this was something to focus on/ have fun with. Through that story telling it became apparent to me that I should really find out if I was adopted.

I did a simple DNA test with my mother's hair and my cheek swab. The results came back that I was not biologically related to my mother. This led to hiring a CI and then to finding Lucy, Kathy's second daughter.

My background: I was raised in Phoenix, AZ and went

to high school at Paradise Valley High. I lived with my Mom & Dad (Glenys and Robert Westby) Brother (Robert, who was not adopted) and our grandparents (Dan & Doris Roderick.)

I got married to my high school sweetheart, Mike in 1983.

When I was twenty-two, we had a baby girl, Ashleigh. A year later we moved to Iowa, where my husband is from, for him to finish college. At twenty-four we had a baby boy, Hayden. In about 1996 we moved back to AZ and have been here ever since.

I have done mostly clerical type jobs, but in my heart is children and foster care. We were therapeutic foster parents for about ten years, letting our license lapse in 2005. But, I still keep in contact with all our kiddos and truly loved each and every one. This turned out to be totally ironic since I was in foster care for the first month of my life and didn't even know it!

My mom adopted me when she was forty-four; I turn forty-four....well, tomorrow. So I had forty-four years with her, and I never knew I was adopted until the last couple of months. It's been a roller coaster, which was very hard when I found out that my birth mom, your sister, Kathleen Fay was deceased. Lots of different feelings, worries like, "Who else is deceased?"

It's been so helpful to learn about Kathy, and get a sense of who she was. I know her life was full of challenges and Lucy explained how sad she was about giving me up. All the details and pictures she has shared have helped me so much; I can't even begin to explain. Plus, Kathy and I look very similar based on the pictures I've seen.

So here we are at the end of the year and now my life has taken this amazing turn, which has also affected Lucy's life, I'm sure. It has brought back all the difficult times, the painful memories to the surface. I wish there was some way that didn't have to happen, it's the last thing I want to do, to cause any difficulty.

My greatest hope is that one day I can meet any family member(s) willing to help me put all my "puzzle" pieces together. I also understand that I have two half-brothers and another half-sister, in addition to Lucy. She has been so nice to caution me and I totally appreciate the heads-up with regards to siblings with troubles/challenges. I understand they have made some unfortunate choices. I have written to Jackie, but I'm hesitant to make contact with the boys.

We all have done things that we wish we could do over. I for one wish I would've been more brave with my mother and really pushed the adoption question. I was so sad to find out that Kathy had passed; I just cried and cried because I was too late to meet her. I so wanted to touch her and let her know that I was okay and I had a good life. I know sometimes we do things that we feel are unforgivable and I could have helped with that. I could have thanked her for my life. But here we are, and we can only move forward.

Which brings me to you....(again). I know I am a stranger, but I would love to know anything you may want to share about your sister, my birth mother. Obviously, if there's any information as to who my father was, that would be greatly appreciated. And then I truly would like to get to know you, if that is at all possible. I know family such as us (aunts/uncles/nieces) know one another from the very beginning and I am a complete stranger to you... and not family, but I feel such a strong instinct to try. I have no intention of being a bother or causing trouble. I don't need anything other than the possibility of learning more about my birth parents. I sort of feel like I've been dropped down into the middle of a mystery! However, I respect you and will just wait to hear from you.

As odd as it is for all of us, I do believe that things hap-
pen for a reason and I was meant to learn about my roots,
my birth family. I wish you a very Merry Christmas and
know that you are in my thoughts and prayers!
With love and respect,
Your niece, Susan

ABOVE: Auntie May, Glenys
(my mother), Bob holding
e, Dan (my grandfather),
d Doris, a.k.a. "Mom"
y grandmother)

BELOW: The Westbys:
bert and Glenys, Robert
d Susan

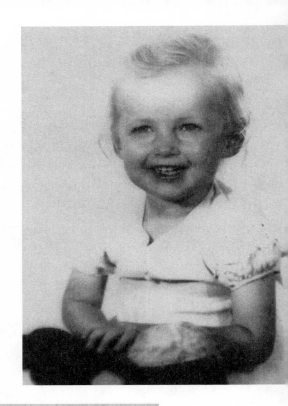

ABOVE: Kathy, one year old

BELOW: Susan, three months

ABOVE: Kathy, age twelve

BELOW: Susan, age twelve

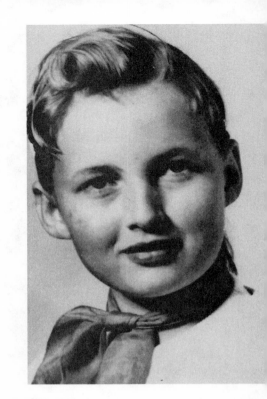

ABOVE: Kathy, age fifteen

BELOW: Susan, age fifteen

CHAPTER 9

Family at Christmastime

"In every conceivable manner, the family is link to our past, bridge to our future."

—Alex Haley

ON THE NIGHT OF DECEMBER 23, the phone rang and I rushed to see the name on the caller ID. It displayed RICHTER, JANE, and I thought, *I don't know anyone named Jane. Ah well, you never know.*

"Hello?" I answered.

"Is this Susan?" asked a man with a deep gravelly voice.

"Yes, this is Susan. Who's this?"

"I'm your Uncle Davey, Susan, and I just got your letter and wanted to call."

"Oh, wow, thank you for calling me! I'm so glad that I get to hear your voice."

"Well, Jane and I live out in the country, and something inside told me to drive to the post office one more time before Christmas. So, I took the old truck out in the snow and went to the station. I opened my box and there was your card. I started to read it in the truck, and as soon as I opened the card and saw the picture on top, I thought of my sister, Kathy. That's how I remember her, the same way you looked when you were young—a beautiful blonde-haired, blue-eyed girl."

My entire being filled with warmth and contentment over this family connection. We talked for over an hour, and again I took detailed notes. It was a new day with new hope, and appropriately, a newly sharpened No. 2 pencil.

Uncle Davey explained how all his siblings had been married several times, and how most of them didn't have their heads screwed on straight, including himself. "I've got it right this time, but oh my dear, it has taken me a long time," he said in a light-hearted way.

Davey stammered while trying to share with me that his parents didn't do a very good job raising the kids, especially the girls. He thought that his mother was mentally ill. He told me, "Now, my sister—your mother, Kathy—she was a sweetheart. It was so sad but everything fell apart for her after she gave birth to you. Please now, don't you feel bad about that. It was her own job to take care of herself once she was an adult."

That hurt so much to hear, but I wanted, I needed the truth. "Thank you for being honest with me," I said.

I shared that I knew about his sisters and brother and asked how they were and if he kept in touch. He tried to remember the last time he had seen his siblings, but only offered the period of "more than a few years ago."

On most holidays, he spoke with one sister, Leslie. Uncle Davey explained, "She's a good gal and really a good sister. She lives in Michigan now, and the others, well…let's just say it hasn't worked out."

When it came to David Sr., his dad, he had nothing but admiration. "He was basically abused as well by my ma. She was controlling and had him under her thumb. But deep down, he was a good man. Oh, about Dad—has anyone told you that *he* was adopted?"

"No, I didn't know that he was adopted." *Cool… Incredible*, I thought.

"Yes, he was actually born in the New York City area. But, he was put on a train and sent across the country, then adopted by the Bardlows. They had a large farm in South Dakota, and through their church and a children's program, they adopted him as a young boy. He told me all about it."

"Wow, that's amazing. So he was on the Orphan Train. I've read books on the subject, but I'd love to hear about your dad's journey."

"Well, it was your grandfather's journey as well," he reminded me. "It was sure something. He had a brother and a sister who were orphans in New York."

"Did they all get put on the train?" I asked.

"Dad told me that 'Sis' wasn't on the train, but I'm not sure why. Maybe someone else wanted her in New York, I can't say. But it wasn't long once they boarded the train that he lost track of his younger brother, Thomas.

"They arrived in Iowa and the children from all the train cars were herded off the train to a place called the sale barn." He asked, "You familiar with those barns, Hon?"

I answered, "Uncle Davey, my husband's family had a sale barn and his grandmother ran a small café alongside. They bought and sold cattle there. There was a big arena in the center and then, rising up all around like an old stadium, were seats made of wooden planks."

"Why yes, that sounds right," Uncle Davey replied. "The children were all led to the big arena by way of metal pathway or chutes. They were single file going in and then lined up in rows. Dad said that he looked and scanned the kids for his brother but never did see him."

"Wow, I imagine that they were brought there so they could be looked at by the parents wanting to adopt, right?"

"Yes, but some had tags sewn into their jackets—they were already spoken for. The rest were checked over, and people took the child they wanted. My dad, your grandfather, was pretty special; he had a tag." Uncle Davey spoke with pride.

"They must have really wanted him. They probably gave him a really good life, right?"

"Well, yes, but not right away. Dad once told me the story about his new family. They lived in Miller, South Dakota, and for the first few months he was downright sad, said he wanted to die. You know, he'd been told that he was going on the railroad out west with his brother so they could get new parents, but that's not how it happened. He was put to work right off the bat, with never a mention of his brother. And he was just a young fella, about six years old, I believe."

I felt so sad for this man, my grandfather—put to work when he was only hoping for a mom and a dad. "Was he abused?" I asked.

"No, oh no, not at all. Let me tell you his story, if you have time. Are you up for that?"

"Oh, I'd love it! I have time, go right ahead." I couldn't wait to hear about my grandfather, my birth grandfather. It felt like I was settling down to read my favorite book; contentment climbed right in. My previous plans for the evening were happily derailed.

My Uncle Davey shared everything he'd been taught about the Orphan Train, and how the Children's Aid Society planned to relocate hundreds of thousands of orphaned children from the late 1800's to the late 1920's. One of those orphaned children who lived in New York City was my grandfather, David.

I can see him now…a sturdy boy, brave, strong, and with a serious face. But tender on the inside, maybe he carried a favorite stuffed bear he got from his mom. One that he hid from the rest of the world.

David never knew his father, but his mother died from infection after his little sister was born. Children's Aid Society took them: David (my grandfather), his brother Thomas, and Sis, his baby sister, were placed in the shelter and given care and beds. It became very crowded and in a few months' time, the three beds had to be stacked on top of one another. Thomas, though only four, was stout, just like David. Many nights the two boys huddled around Sis to comfort her and ease her crying. She was a small child with a spark, a crimson star-shaped birthmark on her cheek and a bright personality for only being two years old. Aid workers, nurses, and many adults often milled around the little girl, as she had a certain magnetism. It was obvious, even to the boys, that everyone wanted to adopt Sis, because she was something special.

David prayed every night they could all stay together, but it wasn't meant to be.

After the rail journey westward and arriving at his new family's farm, David only wanted to be good and do right. He did what was asked of him, ate when he was told, slept when they turned out the light, and got dressed when they woke him in the morning. He knew his sister was fine, but the pain of losing his brother grew and a deep sadness enveloped him over not having a mother and father.

His discontent mounted steadily like steam in a kettle. One morning when the woman of the house pushed him out the door with the other farm hands, he blew.

"Stop pushing me!" David screamed.

"Boy, I push everyone. There's work to be done, son."

As tears dropped like falling stars, he wailed, "I'm not your son!"

His new mother walked out onto the porch and waved on the workers to continue with their chores. She put her arm around David and said, "Come on back inside and sit a spell. We need to talk."

"Yes, ma'am." With his chin to his chest, David slunk in and sat on the edge of a kitchen chair.

"You must despise all of us—your folks for sending you and us for putting you to work." Mrs. Bardlow leaned across the table with her head down trying to make eye contact with David.

"No, ma'am, don't know my folks, only Mrs. Phelps at Children's Aid Society."

"Well, where did you live, David?" she asked, very confused.

"In a big room, ma'am. I was top bunk, my brother Thomas was middle, and Sis on the bottom."

"David, the letter that came with you said you were an only child, and that your parents put you on the train because they were poor and couldn't care for you."

"No, no ma'am, that ain't true." As he thought about his brother Thomas, his best friend, David battled his tears by holding his eyelids shut tight.

As Mrs. Bardlow continued to ask questions, she began to understand David's plight. He was not an angry boy, he was a sad boy. Pushing and shoving, as she did with everyone, only caused his sadness to grow, like fertilizing crops.

"Oh boy, come over here to me," Mrs. Bardlow held her arms open wide. "Tell me all about your dear family. I want to know everything."

She held David close while his anguish flowed out like molten lava. Hot anger at first, and then followed by smoldering sadness. David rid himself of all the pain from the previous months. It was all out, and finally he was cool and calm.

Mrs. Bardlow knew this was the best time to start fresh with her young son. "Boy, we're going fishin' today, just me and you. Run upstairs now and put some shorts on."

David wiped his face and rubbed at his eyes. He looked at her in disbelief.

"Go on," she said. "Work clothes aren't for fishin'."

David smiled at her, his spirit lifted, and he raced up the stairs two at a time. He felt cleansed and cared for, and thought, *Wow, what a wonderful idea—fishing. I don't know how to do it, but I'm goin' fishin'.*

As they climbed into the Ford truck with their fishing poles and picnic basket, Mrs. Bardlow called out to her husband, "Henry, David and I are going out to the lake today."

Rushing out of the feed shed, Henry asked, "Who ya got with ya?"

"David, your son…we're gonna do some fishing."

In that moment, David let out a sigh. That's what he wanted more than anything, to be someone's son.

As the months passed, the loss of his brother and sister faded somewhat, but the pain never fully left his heart. David had a great appreciation for Henry and Betty Bardlow, his new parents, and loved them for adopting him.

"Susan, my dad really loved his parents. When I was a boy, we visited many times and they were just great to me. I'll never forget the last time we made the trip—it was just before my grandmother passed away. She gave my dad a letter she had saved over all those years. Susan, I'll send you a copy, it's darned near incredible."

"I'd love to see anything you have to share. I'm so glad that worked out for him, because his beginnings were dreadful. It seems like once the truth was out, both he and his mother could start over. And then, it was all about family and love." After I said the words, I chuckled inside. I thought, *Oh how I try to wrap things up nice and neat.*

Uncle Davey said, "Now if you don't mind me sayin', maybe that's why he wasn't so concerned about his girls giving up their babies for adoption." Then he asked, "You did know that Leslie gave up a baby, too?"

"Yes, Lucy told me about it. She didn't remember when her mother told her, but at some point she shared how they'd both lost babies. I guess Kathy and Leslie had babies just about two years apart from one another," I continued. "This means there's a Bardlow cousin of mine out there who's adopted."

"I suppose so. Dad thought he did real well by adoption. We never talked about my sisters openly, nor did they ever speak about it—that I heard. But I know my dad drove them to the next town before their babies came. He drove them, not my mother. And they seemed to do okay, I guess."

I'm not sure if he was beginning to feel uncomfortable, but he changed the subject and asked, "Susan, have you talked to anyone else in the family?"

"Well, Lucy—but that's it. I sent letters to Sharon, Leslie, you and the youngest two, Denise and Stephen. Oh and Lucy's sister, Jackie, but not her brothers. I understand that Jackie and the boys have had some troubles with drugs; Lucy told me."

"Oh yes. I knew that from when Kathy was still alive. She didn't get along very well with them or her sisters. Kathy had a big falling out with everyone, especially Denise. She was about eight years younger and you know what? Kathy told me that Denise slept with her husband! I think the other two gals took Denise's side—she claimed that she didn't want to be with him but that he was forceful. After the dust settled, Denise went off with some other guy. Now I hear she's with another fella. They're into this hocus pocus stuff, you know, chasing after spirits in peoples' houses and claiming to be psychic with *oooh* special powers."

Wow, such interesting information and some bizarre stuff too, I thought.

Uncle Davey went on to ask about my family. He was curious about who had adopted me, his niece and he listened intently. Neither of us could understand or figure out why I wasn't told of the adoption. However, we both found it wonderfully ironic that Sis, his aunt (his dad's baby sister) and I both have birthmarks on our face.

I told him, "I hope she had an easier time with it than I did. Kids were cruel to me and my parents didn't handle it right, either. But, I have to share that even though I despised it, Mike found it particularly interesting, and he named my birthmark 'Sparky.'"

"Yes, and my dad described Sis's birthmark as a spark from a star."

Finally, my birthmark was interesting and I felt like it made me special, along with my grandfather's beloved baby sister. I never thought I'd see the day where I felt proud to have a birthmark. I savored every word about our specialness from this kind man who sounded like an old cowboy from the wild west.

We went on to discuss the places I had lived, and I told what I knew about my beginnings, and how my parents and brother had lived in the White Mountains.

"Oh, you don't say?" Davey asked. "Where exactly did they live?"

"The White Mountain area, Pinetop and Show Low. They had a couple of businesses actually. For years they ran summer cabin rentals called the Broken Arrow Lodge. They built it from the ground up and lived on the property too. The other business was a liquor store; my dad bought that and was the owner/operator. They sold the lodge and moved closer into Show Low, but ran the liquor store for years. That about covers it all, until the year I was born."

Davey hesitated for a moment. "Susan, I would not be a bit surprised if my mother knew your mother. Every summer they rented cabins and spent time up north as far back as I can remember. My dad loved the White Mountain area, especially the fishing. They stayed in Pinetop and Show Low every summer, and even the summer my sister was pregnant. I remember her chubby belly being an issue with my mom. Maybe they struck up a conversation and knew Kathy was pregnant. I wouldn't be a bit surprised if my mother made the arrangements."

"Uncle Davey, my folks lived with my grandparents, Dan and Doris Roderick. Do you remember them, or my mother's name, Glenys, or my dad's liquor store, Bob's Liquors?" I asked. The thought of being able to connect some dots was a thrill.

"Oh, Hon. I don't, but it sure would make sense."

To which I agreed. There was no reason my parents would use an adoption agency in Tucson, in the southern part of the state, when they lived in northern Arizona—unless they knew someone having a baby in Tucson. *Aha*, I thought. But that was all he knew.

We had a wonderfully friendly visit, but finally, there wasn't much left to say. We both said we'd like to chat again, but neither one has called the other. It was great to hear his voice and learn some incredible things, but again—we are but strangers with a genetic connection, which leaves us still as strangers.

By now, those with a more common niece-uncle relationship would have years of holidays and special events in their shared history. He had my picture, but that was it, and one picture does not make a relationship. Honestly, in this case, with this person, I wish it did. I'd love to spend more time with my Uncle Davey and his wife. Maybe someday.

He did send me a copy of the letter saved by Mrs. Bardlow, telling about his dad's placement via the Orphan Train. It began with strict instructions followed by an explanation of the transaction. Here is little David's orphan letter:

HAVE THE NUMBER ON THIS
NOTICE OF ARRIVAL WITH YOU
WHEN THE TRAIN ARRIVES.

NOTICE OF ARRIVAL
Number 26
Mr. Henry Bardlow of Miller, South Dakota
Arrival, Mason City, Iowa
No. 26, boy—orphan, only child.

We take pleasure in notifying you that the little boy which
you so kindly ordered will arrive at Manley, Rock Island
Train on Thursday, June 24th on the train due to arrive at
5:15 a.m. We ask that you kindly be at Mason City Iowa
Sale Barn to receive the child at 9 a.m. Please be 30 minutes early to avoid any possibility of missing collection, as
the child may be placed in the open group of children to
be adopted.

The name of the child, date of birth, and name and
address of party to who the child is assigned will be found
sewn in the coat of the boy.

Bring your number along with the arrival information with you. A copy of proof of your home address is to
be given up in exchange for the child who will also have
a corresponding number to yours.

Yours very truly,
Mrs. Phelps, Sisters of Charity

Also included was a photocopy of a small piece of fabric. It was
difficult to read, but it identified David as an orphan, and listed
his date of birth, along with the name of the party to collect him:
Mr. and Mrs. H. Bardlow.

There was no mention of his siblings nor of the name of his
mother. There was no last name at all, which eerily reminds me
of my struggle to find my father and his first or last name. Over
a century apart, and in totally different circumstances, both of

us experienced challenges under the adoption cloud of secrecy.

Uncle Davey's stories were rich with his family history—our family history, and he seemed to enjoy sharing it with me. I loved learning about the beginnings of the Bardlow family that were ultimately my beginnings. At least there was someone in my family who was adopted, my birth grandfather, and I was happy to have this in common with him. From my hill of difficulty looking towards his mountain of hardship, it was easy for me to feel his grace and capacity for love. This, a glimpse through the window of history, was a great gift.

But sometimes stories are filtered through glass so clouded with dirt and debris that it's difficult to follow or discern the truth.

Other family members made some of their history known to me with reckless abandon, displaying their childhood through panes that were cracked, chipped, even bloodstained. Their words were surreal and evoked their unstable lives.

I received one reply to my letters by standard mail. This was the day after Christmas from my Aunt Leslie. Leslie was Kathy's closest sister and friend, being just two years older. According to family, she also placed a baby up for adoption when she was eighteen. I hoped that she would feel compassion for me and possibly share everything that Lucy could not—most importantly, who Kathy dated and fell in love with the first part of 1964.

Leslie's letter was gloomy, hand-written, and many pages long. She did share a sweet story about how she and Kathy had fun doing simple things in the front yard. She wrote about a dancing game, and how they'd spin and jive until a car came by, then abruptly freeze. Her letter had different types of pages, the first several on stationary, and some on copy paper. It seemed to span a few days. The last page was rumpled. It was all in printing rather than cursive, but the ink was distorted by what looked like many tear drops. However, her pain was evident on each page and through every sentence in her letter. I could feel her sadness even in a pleasant story. She never mentioned being pregnant, or even being around Kathy when she was pregnant with me. Leslie claimed to have no idea who my birth father was.

Her letter ended by saying that she most likely would not be contacting me again. "Don't take it personal, but some things need to be left in the past," she wrote. And that's the last I've heard from my Aunt Leslie.

I also received returned mail from the post office. My half-sister Jackie apparently didn't pick up or accept my letter, as it was stamped, UNCLAIMED MAIL.

The next time I spoke to Lucy I mentioned the returned mail, to which she replied, "Susan, Jackie is so excited and has been waiting for her letter! Can you send it again?"

She went on to describe how her sister's apartment was in a bad part of town and people often stole letters, especially around Christmas, thinking there might be money inside. This didn't make sense to me, since the letter was returned, not lost or stolen. She simply didn't pick it up. But, I thought, *Lucy really wants me to try again, so I will.*

Because Jackie had struggled with drug addiction, I wasn't sure what to think. I sort of felt like I was off the hook when I got the returned mail. *It'll be fine*, I convinced myself, and I wrote another letter with the attitude—let's just see what happens. The envelope had my return address on it, and I also decided to give her my email address. With that being the most I could do, I double-checked her address and sent my letter.

About a week later on, New Year's Day, I got a call in the evening. "Susan, hi! This is your sister Jackie." I was dazed, I didn't even get *hello* out all the way.

"Oh hi, you must have gotten my letter," I said awkwardly, thinking, *I hoped you would write back or email, not call me.*

"Yeah, but I'm not a letter writer so I searched and tried to find your phone number but it's unlisted, so Lucy finally gave it to me. I found a number but it was wrong and Lucy didn't want me to call some other family member or something. I am calling you to tell you that you have a sister and I love you." She ran all the words together and then gasped, sucking in a big breath of air. She sounded almost frantic.

"Oh, right…" I didn't really know what to say; she came across so odd to me. "Yeah…um, I grew up with an older brother and now I have two sisters and two more brothers, it's pretty amazing."

Jackie's voice was raspy, like a pack-a-day smoker—deeper than I expected, and nothing like Lucy's. She spoke quickly, almost frantically, often speaking right over me. I quickly got out my note pad and was ready for her information and anything she had to share about my newfound family.

"Susan, I want to tell you I've been waiting for you. I don't have anybody and I don't know what Lucy has told you but we ain't close."

"Really? Lucy said that you guys got together for your birthday just a few weeks ago and you went shopping, had lunch and…."

Jackie interrupted, "Well, let me tell you, she has done so many things to hurt me and after everything I went through for her when we were growing up, I can't stand her anymore! The only thing that helped me was that I had a doll, and you know what I named her? Susan. I named all my dolls Susan, after you."

Okay, well there was no way she could have known my adopted name, I thought. *But, I'll go along and ask about her childhood.* "What happened when you were growing up?"

"Well, I used to stand in front of Lucy and take her beatings. Susan, so much went on and after getting your letter, it all came back. I'm even having nightmares again. You know no one loves me in my family? Not no one. Did you know that child services took my daughter, Stacie? And that bitch Lucy wouldn't take her in. No one cares about me. Oh, I have my kids, they are right with me now—Stacie, Lee, and my boy, Lonny. I'll always have them and no one's taking them away. But the others, they don't love me."

"Oh they don't? You mean Lucy too? She told me that you guys are close, and—"

"Well, Ted, my brother, he is just a user and he's into crack and all these other things, and Leo we haven't heard from in years. Ted is bad, you know? He's had about five kids and the state has taken them all away. You know it's because of him that our mother died, right?"

I thought, *wait—hold on.* "What? Ted had something to do with Kathy's death? Lucy didn't say anything about that."

Jackie began to sob, and at first I couldn't understand a thing she said. I held the phone out away from my ear and looked at it in disbelief. *Oh my, this is my half-sister. Why did I send the letter that second time? This is a nightmare!*

Finally, I could make out the words. Jackie said, "Did you know that she died on top of my daughter, Stacie? Oh, it was horrible, we was all using and Susan, she died!"

There were more tears and sobs, even setting the phone down to cough. Then she went on, "I told Lucy it wasn't my fault. Ted was doing horrible things to her and she took all these pills."

Her voice dropped into a monotone, "You know, like he had sex with her when she was out of it and she didn't know who he was." Then horribly, she began to laugh!

I grimaced and held the receiver tightly. I wondered if she was serious, or insane, or if this was all a very cruel joke.

"Oh yeah, Susan, he was on top of her and she would just moan. Teddy told me, 'She liked it.'" Jackie laughed again and spoke to imitate his voice, "'Oh, *you* feel so good.' Teddy made fun of the whole thing, but I don't think Mom really knew what was going on," she said.

"What?"

"Yeah," she continued. "It was just messed up, but I didn't really know what was going on either."

It sure sounded like she knew what was going on. I was extremely uncomfortable listening to her. I thought, *who is this person?* And most of the time I could only manage to utter, "*What?*" I was in total disbelief. Maybe I was trying to convince myself that I misunderstood. I could only say, "*What?*" over and over again. I swear, I could feel my skin crawl.

Jackie took a deep breath, and her rapid-pace chatter grew. "Susan, when she died I was in the bathtub and I could hear stuff going on and Stacie was calling me, 'Mom…Mom…Mom.' When I opened the door, there Mom was on top of Stacie and she wasn't moving. My little girl was pinned under my mother.

Stacie was …uh, I don't know, about six years old then, and she was freaking out. She was a little girl and I had to push Mom off of her and onto the floor. She was so heavy, and had Stacie pinned down."

Jackie laughed and laughed as she continued the story. "And after Mom went thud—down on the floor, Teddy cracked up and couldn't stop laughing. Stacie even stopped crying and started laughing. Everyone was just laughing!"

"*What?*" I had never been so mortified. I spoke very clearly and deliberately. "Jackie, I can't do this. This is very upsetting to me and you need to stop. You need to take things slower."

For once, it was quiet on the other end of the line. I said, gently, "Maybe you can write to me and we can start over and get to know each other. There are so many things flying around in my head, like your story of how our mother died—and one issue I have is that you're telling me this stuff, talking loud right in front of your kids. I can hear them in the background. I have spent most of my life caring for kids, I was a foster parent for years and…."

It was no surprise, but Jackie interrupted one last time. "Well I don't write. Lucy told you stuff about me, didn't she? I knew you wouldn't like me, I knew this would happen. That is just fine, you won't ever hear from me again!"

With dramatic flair, she shouted, "I'm out!" Then I heard *CRASH, BAM!* as the phone hit a wall or the floor or some hard object and we were disconnected.

Thank God! I thought. I've never been so relieved to end a call. I stood there, deeply upset, seething as I felt myself become hot with anger. There was only one thing to do. I decided to find out the truth about this infuriating woman who was my half-sister.

I immediately went into the office and emailed Lucy about Jackie's call. She replied the next morning, and sadly, all the horrible, dysfunctional things I had heard were true. We emailed back and forth and she filled me in on her childhood and other things about her family. Lucy didn't share the details but she ran away when she was sixteen, never to return. She told me that her older brother Ted had always been a sexual predator, and she worried that Stacie was being sexually abused. The more information I got the worse I felt. I was worlds away from first learning of my birth mother, whom I had so empathized with for her deep sadness of losing a baby. I couldn't even imagine how upsetting this all was for Lucy. She had lived it and then repeated it for me. I was a universe away from my sweet grandfather who had traveled on the Orphan Train. However, Lucy was honest and shared the truth, and there wasn't much else I could ask for.

My compassion slowly drained, and I thought, *I can't believe this is where I came from.* The level of dysfunction was inconceivable to me. I felt like I had been lying in muck with bugs and worms crawling all over me. I'd never felt this way in my life before.

Lucy tried to soften the blow and was kind enough to tell me, "You are the best thing that ever happened to my mother and I mean that in all sincerity. You are a good person and you've cared for so many people. You got all that was good in Mom."

Lucy and I both have had our struggles and miscommunications, and we will probably never meet. At least that's how it feels right now. Within the first six months of emailing and talking, it was painfully clear; I brought back all the sorrow and regret of a broken relationship between her, her mother, and her sister. I was simply a reminder of the part of her life she was trying to leave behind and forget. And she had been doing quite well until I came along. I imagined that I became the festering family thorn in her side, causing the buildup of emotional misery.

I used to email Lucy at least once a week and share news about my family and kids, how and what we were all doing. I believe "Low-Self-Esteem-Susan" was hoping to find someone who needed her. At first, Lucy shared her feelings and let me into her life, but it didn't last long. After a few months, her responses were always that she was too busy—too busy to comment or respond. And most often when I asked questions about our mother's dreams, life plans, or relationships with other family, Lucy told me she had no idea.

Finally, after knowing her for almost a year, I gave up and stopped annoying her with all my pesky emails. I did want a relationship with Lucy, and I always wanted a sister. However, it was obvious there was a problem and at the end of the day, we were in fact just strangers. And I wanted her to have peace. I in no way represent any sort of peace for her. We are in our forties, and even though we have this biological connection, we have no shared history. I do hold out hope for the day we can reconnect, become friends, and maybe even sisters. I would love to look forward with her and be finished with the past.

I am eternally grateful for Lucy's time that Thanksgiving evening and for all the pictures and stories. She gave me the truth that I needed to move on and move forward. I did ask many questions in preparation for this book and although she never communicated her feelings about it, I felt the contempt in the four words she consistently used in her replies to me: "I have no idea."

While some bits of our history are welcome, life is not always so comfortable. It is multi-faceted and often shot through with darkness. Yes, it's a darkness I never expected to find, but that's the way it goes. You take the good with the bad, and sometimes you must wallow in the mire of an ugly truth.

A truth, nonetheless.

CHAPTER 10

Home Movies

"If you don't know your family's history, then you don't know anything. You are a leaf that doesn't know it is part of a tree."
— Michael Crichton

SOME DAYS THE MAIL IS FULL OF GARBAGE; and then, when you least expect it, it can change your life. At least how you feel about your life, anyway. I requested my non-identifying information from the adoption agency that had handled my adoption. I was hesitant because so many adoptees receive very little information, and what they do learn leads to more questions than answers. The person I dealt with in Arizona seemed sympathetic to my situation and told me she would send everything she could. In my mind, she ought to be able to send everything, since my adoptive parents were deceased and my birth mom had passed away years ago. Whose privacy was left to protect? I wanted to be hopeful for what she'd send, but I realistically assumed the worst and planned to receive very little.

I had in my hand the envelope from the adoption agency, and it wasn't small or thin. I opened it, and there were fifteen pages about my birth family, my birth, and my adoptive family's home study. I was ecstatic; I sat taller, held the pages tightly, and began to read about my birth mother and her family. I was starved for information and this was the sustenance I'd yearned for.

Here is the redacted information provided to me by the adoption agency:

The social worker first met with the birth mom on October 21, 1964. She describes her as tall, slender, and blonde, with soft blue eyes and a full mouth. She seemed uncomfortable and shy during the first meeting. They discussed her doctor visit. Things were explained to her, and she didn't have any questions other than how often they would meet. On the next visit, she also did not seem much inclined to talk. At first, the doctor thought she might be carrying twins and the birth mom did not know why that bothered her, but it did. The social worker determined part of her concern was just not knowing anything about the birthing process, and she explained it to her in detail. She also offered the birth mom the opportunity to tour the hospital, and she said she had never been hospitalized before and that might be helpful. She did say she felt better, as she had been worried about how painful the birth would be. This was understandable, since the birth mom was young, just eighteen years old.

The social worker told the birth mom she thought she was more bothered in her feelings about the pregnancy than she wanted to appear. Birth mom said it worried her that she could not keep the baby, but she thought placement was best. She felt very emotional about the baby and really wanted to keep it, but she did not have the support of the father or of her parents. Her mother insisted that she give the baby up if the father wouldn't marry her. It hurt her that the father did not want to marry her and that she wanted to hate him, but couldn't. They had talked about marriage but when she told him she was pregnant, he seemed uninterested. The social worker noted that it had been some time since the birth mom had seen the father, because he had been in jail; and then when she saw him again she told him she was pregnant. In spite of his lack of interest, they agreed to marry and started making plans. A few days later, he visited the home and told her and her parents he felt he was too young to marry and support a family. He even asked her if she was sure it was his baby. The family decided not to press the marriage since he was unwilling. She said it really hurt when he accused her of having relations with someone else. She discussed this relationship with social workers at length and agreed he might not have been the best man to marry; and because of his past, her parents didn't think he was suitable. His past included dropping out of school, drinking, getting in trouble with the law, and having come from a broken home. She also reported they had only been intimate one time. The birth mom was very uncomfortable around her mother, often speaking in a soft whisper directly to social worker.

As time went by, they discussed how hard it was for her to think of not being with her family at Christmas. In addition, when she thought about the baby she thought how hard it would be to give the baby up, even though she believed that it was best, so she tried not to think about it. However, she had no choice and felt her parents controlled this decision. She was debating whether she wanted to see the baby or not when it was born. She was afraid to, but the worker encouraged her to do so.

On December 18 the worker got the call that the baby was born. She went to the hospital, but the birth mom was in recovery and she could not see her. After the birth, her parents were insistent she be back home before the twenty-fourth, and she returned home before the worker could see her as she was on vacation. Another worker handled the adoption paperwork.

The birth mom signed consent to the adoption on December 22, 1964, after her mother showed up insisting that things move along and her daughter be home for the holidays.

Follow-up meetings with the social worker were declined for a multitude of reasons. The birth mom's mother finally wrote a letter stating that her daughter was in the hospital for severe pain, possibly a kidney stone, and that she, the mother, was writing on her behalf. She claimed that her daughter didn't need to meet with a social worker and that she had gotten a job at the phone company and would be moving forward once she was well, putting the whole dreadful experience behind her. No further contact was made.

Oh my poor dear birth mother, I thought. I put my hands flat on the pages, thinking of her face. "Sweet girl, you did want me so very much," I said aloud.

I had so many feelings about her mother, my grandmother, and the lack of parental support. Based on the social worker's notes, Kathy clearly had more to say—what I'd seen was only the tip of the iceberg. I was deeply disappointed by how her mother had forced her into adoption, making it the only option. My mother did not want to give away her baby! She wanted me. I palpably felt her love for her child from the words of strangers, written so long ago. Yes, the pregnancy was a mistake. I was an accident, but nonetheless special and no less a miracle.

According to the information, I began my life with the Westbys, my adoptive family, on January 12, 1965. They had been ready for me since my birth on December 18, but placement wasn't finalized for more than three weeks. Those early weeks of my life were spent in a foster home. The irony of my having been in a foster home is spectacular! I smile thinking of it. Yet, I feel uneasy as the information settled in. *Who took care of me? Was I loved?*

In anticipation of the placement (my adoption), the Westby family moved down from the White Mountain area at the end of October and rented an apartment in central Phoenix.

The county recorder's Web site provided me with the address for my birth mother and her family, and the adoption agency listed the address for my parent's apartment.

Hmm, I thought. *I know where they both lived when I was born. They don't seem to have been very far apart from one an-*

other. Interesting—I wonder if the house and the apartment are still there?

When my birth mom returned home on December 23, she lived with her family less than a mile from my adoptive family's apartment. My birth mother's home is still there, a modest brick house in what was once a nice neighborhood. I can envision Kathy and Leslie twirling and playing in the front yard. My mind fills in the details of a wonderful family-oriented area. Now, it's right down the street from a new freeway. It's loud and a few homes on the street are vacant. Less than a minute away, I found the apartment my folks had rented. I recognized the front architecture from pictures I'd seen. There's one of my brother with his new toy trucks on the front patio, playing between wrought-iron posts on Christmas Day, 1964. And there they were right in front of me; the same posts as in the pictures. I had lived with my new adoptive family in that apartment for three months, until my family bought a home in the area. My heartbroken birth mother was less than a mile away, with no idea that her baby girl was so close.

I cannot begin to explain how strange it was to visit both places—to see where both my families had lived. The Bardlow home, where I had lived inside my mother, and then the small apartment where I had first lived with the Westbys, my new and future family.

The agency had done a home study on my adoptive family and that report was sent to me as well. As I read it, a calm peacefulness came over me. There were things that instantly reminded me of my folks and grandparents. I felt wanted and loved by my adoptive family. At the time I was adopted my brother was almost six years old. He didn't understand how babies come into the world, that the mother has a large belly that grows with the infant inside. He thought all new parents drive to another town and pick up their baby. As he got older, he never connected the strange circumstances of how I came to be a part of the family with adoption. I was just his sister.

In her report, the social worker noted many times how my

brother was enamored of me. She wrote, "He's very proud to have his own baby sister."

While writing *our book* my mother told me the details of the long car ride home. However, much of the focus was on my brother. She told me the trip had occurred when I was two days old, but I can only assume this was the journey home from the adoption agency and I was close to a month old.

When Mother told me about the trip, she was full of excitement, on the edge of her seat. She recalled how thrilled my brother was, saying, "We could hardly contain him. Bobby was bouncing up and down in the back seat before you and I even got in the car. His dad told him, 'Now, settle down,' and he'd manage to sit still for about five seconds, and then he'd start again. As we got on the highway, you were sound asleep in my arms and I said, 'Okay guys, what are we going to name her?'

"Oh, Bob was jubilant and he squealed, 'Oh I know a name, I have lots of good names, Momma!'"

In the middle of her story I thought, *You waited until we were on the way home to start thinking of a name for me?* Adopted or not, the prospect of that was confusing to me. Babies are given a name while at the hospital.

I asked, "So did Bob name me?"

"Oh no. He was giving us name after name and his voice was getting louder, so I told him that if he sat still and whispered, he could hold you in the back seat and think of a name. We had to have some peace and quiet; it was a long ride home. I handed you back to him all bundled up, and your head was on his chest with your body resting on him and his legs. He hunched up his shoulders and put his arms around you. I told your dad, 'Look at this; you have to see your son.'

"Your dad moved the rear-view mirror, tilting it down so he could see Bob. His eyes were the size of saucers and he was grinning ear to ear."

"So what was Bob's name that he liked?" I asked.

"Oh he was stuck on Kim. 'Kimberly, Momma, let's call her Kimberly,' he said. I finally told him that we would think about it and that was a nice name." She told me every word she could remember about Bobby's reaction.

That's the most I know about my homecoming. My mother never shared any other details that I could grab hold of as part of my beginnings.

It wasn't until I reviewed all the information from the adoption agency that the pieces of my story, the ones I already held, became clearer. Like a rare book, I treasure each word from the agency, and have re-read them again and again. To me, this was like finding your baby book or scrapbook from when you were born, listing the details of *you*—the one that you never knew existed.

In the placement notes, I found that the agency people had visited with my parents several times.

MSW Karen reported:

When the Westbys came in they were obviously excited and overjoyed to be getting their baby girl. They told me how anxious they had been, particularly during the past month since we had given them some hope that a placement would be made sooner. Bobby insisted they put up the crib three months ago so when they got the word about the baby they had no preparations to make. They were more than ready on all fronts.

Mr. Westby told me since Bobby will be in school they feel he would have a better chance in a larger system, which is why they moved from the White Mountains. He also bought a hardware and variety store in Phoenix, which he will operate. They are currently looking for a home to purchase in the Phoenix area near the store.

I provided Adopting Parents' Responsibilities form and after they both read it, they stated they had no questions. I mentioned that the form is to be signed after placement and after making their final decision on adopting. Mr. Westby said, "You don't think you are going to get her back now, do you?"

I have no doubt this couple had already made up their mind, saying that she was a perfect fit, and Mrs. Westby's parents were delighted to have a baby granddaughter, as well.

First pre-hearing visit Social Worker Mary reported:

Mrs. Westby was at home when I arrived, and her husband, son, and parents were expected shortly. Without hesitation, she began to tell me how wonderful Susan is, what a delight to have, and that everyone comments on her beauty. Mrs. Westby was very pleased with Susan's looks, blonde hair, and blue eyes. She pointed out that the baby still has a reddish discoloration on her chin but that when she had the baby looked at by the doctor he advised that it would most likely disappear. She described it as looking more like a rash than a birthmark. This was an acceptable diagnosis to her.

Mrs. Westby's parents arrived and this social worker noticed the bond between Mrs. Westby and her parents, especially with her mother. The grandparents were profuse in their praise for Susan and quite accepting of her as their grandchild.

Bobby entered, full of energy and seemingly well identified with his father. He gently loved Susan and asked to hold her. He did so with care and seemed proud of his mother trusting him with such responsibility. Bobby loves to show his new sister off and is very happy to be a big brother.

I feel the County Attorney should be notified and the petition to adopt be signed by the Westbys.

During the final hearing, Lead Social Worker Esther noted:

Susan appeared to be a happy, well-adjusted child. Mrs. Westby held Susan throughout the hearing. She is growing and appears to be in good health. Her blonde hair is coming in slowly but Mrs. Westby is pleased that is appears to be curly. She is also happy that Susan's hair is still blonde. Susan is accommodating her mother in another way in that her eyes are blue. Although Mrs. Westby stated that she was teasing when she specified in her preference for a child a little blue-eyed blonde girl, she is happy that Susan is just that. Mrs. Westby mentioned that the mark on the baby's chin is still present but joked, "We will just have to keep her anyway."

Mrs. Westby states that Susan is now almost 17 pounds, has two teeth, and a third is about to appear. She is sitting by herself and is trying to crawl. At the present time, she is a little puzzled at just how to accomplish this, but both parents state that she is working hard at it. She prefers going it alone, as she brushes them aside if they try to help her. The parents state that it didn't take them long to learn that Susan is rather independent and prefers being alone. Except when it comes to Mrs. Westby's mother, Susan's grandmother.

Through information sources like this one from the adoption agency, I was able to look back into time. I learned about my family's lives before I entered and when they first came into my life. So different from what I was told. But what meant the most is that I now had the opportunity to learn about the true beginning of my existence. You can only fully heal once things are out in the open, and not until then.

The words instantly turned into priceless memories for me. I recalled my dad, Robert Westby, and could see him much younger, being the head of the family and having an attitude of all business. I could well imagine his struggle dealing with an emotional human transaction such as adoption. I could see my grandmother behind the scenes, elated to adopt me, a baby girl. That thought filled me with contentment. Although I was young when she passed away and may not have been able to articulate our relationship, we bonded on a soulful level and she has always been with me.

As I absorbed the words on the page, I saw that my brother was just as I would have imagined him, loving and kind. His affection towards me while growing up was significant. I nestle in the comfort of my very own family movies, each and every time I read the notes from the adoption agency.

It's not perfect, but I finally have my own little slice of heaven. It's so much more fulfilling than non-identifying information.

CHAPTER 11

Marcus House

"When we seek to discover the best in others, we
somehow bring out the best in ourselves."
                                    —*William Arthur Ward*

KATHY SPENT A DECADE IN SILENCE regarding the birth and loss of
her first-born child—me. Only when her sister Denise was almost
eighteen did she discuss the events of that painful time. It was a
discussion my aunt will never forget, but one she agreed to share.

"It hurt so bad to know what my sister went through, so many
years before. I had no idea until our visit how profoundly injured
she was and forever changed," explained Denise.

Kathy was twenty-eight and married with four children when
she spent the day with her little sister who was about to turn eighteen. They went to a park and sat under a huge juniper and talked
for hours. Her goal was, in a roundabout way, to tell Denise not
to have sex. Kathy recalled every upsetting moment and fear so
Denise would heed her warning.

"I was at Marcus House and I remember crying before I went
in, and then I just tried to think about Christmas all the time,
until my water broke that is, and, well… I have never thought of
Christmas in the same way again," Kathy told her sister.

Denise asked, "It hurt when your water broke?"

"Oh no, it was sort of like I peed. It was warm and, well, wet.
But then right after I had horrible pain and I had to sit right down
on the floor. The house mom called the hospital and said it was

time to go. But I had to take everything with me and I wasn't ready. It was early in the morning and it was still dark."

"You didn't have your stuff packed?" Denise asked.

"Oh I had my clothes and everything, but I'd done a lot of paintings and they were on the wall and I wanted to take them down and pack them. The pain was so intense that there wasn't time, and the house mom rushed me out to the car. I wanted to go back and get them, but I never went back, Ma saw to that."

"And when you got to the hospital, the baby was born?"

"Oh, no, not for a long time. When I got there it was about six-thirty a.m. The first thing they did was get me into bed, dressed in a horrible hospital gown, and put in an IV. It hurt a lot, but then I was having contractions, which hurt a lot more. I was crying and calling for help. The doctor came and gave me some medicine in my IV that helped right away and it made me sleep."

"And that's when the baby came out?" Denise asked breathlessly.

"No, I woke up to the most intense pain ever, and they told me to try and breathe deeper. It would last for a while and then I'd fall asleep again until the next pain. Finally they were yelling at me to push, it hurt so bad all around my bottom. Not like in one place, but all over down there. I really lost it, thought I was going to die. Finally, the baby came out and I sorta remember the relief, but then I must have fallen asleep."

"So what did it look like?

"I don't know, at that point. I didn't see the baby until later, about eight o'clock. I was so tired and wanted to see it and find out if it was a boy or girl, but I couldn't even talk."

"Oh yeah, I remember now, you had a girl right?"

"Yes, they brought her to see me all bundled up in a blanket, and the nurse handed her to me and I didn't know what to do. She was fussing, crying a little. I took her and the nurse told me how to hold her and support her head. As soon as the baby was on top of me and I was holding her, she settled right down. I'll never forget…she did this really big yawn, so precious. The nurse said, 'It's a girl and she's perfect and healthy.'

"I felt a horrible sadness welling up inside of me as I looked at her tiny face. Then I started to cry, everything was blurry and my nose was running. The nurse told me that if I was going to get upset she had to take the baby. She tried to take her and I said, 'Okay, okay, I'm fine... I won't cry."

"Did you get to hold her for a long time?"

"I did, I held her for hours and I looked at her fingers and toes. She had the cutest, tiniest ears and super bright blue eyes. Giving up my baby girl was the hardest thing I've ever done."

Denise asked, "Harder than giving birth?"

"It was all hard, being pregnant and loving her and then leaving. Her name was Kay. That's what I named her because they changed my name while I was there to Kay. To think about it now is even sickening. Forced to give up my baby girl, living away from home, Mom and Dad being mad at me, giving birth, and then this tiny baby that I had no idea I would love and had to leave, it was all beyond hard. Sex is supposed to be between two people who want to start a family, not a high school girl afraid of family. Don't you forget that," she said, pointing her finger at Denise.

"But it was so great when you got home for Christmas. I missed you, and I remember being so happy to see you. Even if you were sick...remember?"

"Mom told everyone I was sick. 'Caught a bug,' she said. I was not sick, I was depressed, and I couldn't even look at the stupid Christmas tree. I will never get over leaving my baby and I don't know where she is or if she's okay. I thought having my own would help but it hasn't. Now I feel like a bad mom in addition to dealing with this dreadful loss. It's horrible and it will always be horrible, every Christmas."

And it was horrible. All the things Denise told me about my birth mother and her feelings made me realize she had been devastated. I began to understand that even as years passed and she got better, Christmastime was never the same. Kathy only thought about me, the baby she left at the hospital. Once the seed of guilt was planted, it grew and grew. Guilt was part of her everyday life, and she floundered.

Some of the hospital records were part of my adoption file, and most of the nurses' notes after my birth were included. These notes, along with her sisters' stories, provided great insight and helped me to treasure my birth mother's love, albeit brief. We were together and then, in the blink of an eye, it was over.

Nursing Notes:
- *Birth Mom (BM) held the baby as often as possible, tenderly kissing her face and head.*
- *BM whispered to the baby, "I am sorry, I love you very much and I will always remember you my baby girl."*
- *BM is trying to be brave but seems heartbroken. Cries when baby cries.*
- *Very sad — BM is crying, tears on the baby and on her blanket.*
- *When the baby was taken from her, BM said, "I am so sorry you can't go home with me, but God will be with you." She cried a lot, tears soaked the receiving blanket. She kissed the baby one more time. Sad.*

Realizing I had marinated in my mother's grief for nine months, so much about me becomes clear now. I'm beginning to feel reborn, and I'm keenly focused on learning as much as I possibly can. I feel the power that comes with knowledge.

After hearing the story of my birth and reading the nurses' notes, I felt compelled to locate the maternity home, Marcus House. After many hours of research, I found their address, but now it's Sunland Springs, an assisted living home for the elderly.

I had already located and visited both my birth and adoptive family's homes; only the maternity home visit remained. This was the last stop on the beginning-of-Susan historical tour. The discovery of the home my mother had lived in for three months was exciting. As I drove the two hours toward my destination, I thought about my mother and her fear, her pain, but mostly her familial disappointment. As much as she felt they had let her down, she must have also been ashamed for the trouble she caused.

Arriving in Tucson, I drove up a charming street and found

the address. There it was—the brick walk, the stairs, and the home, waiting for me. I felt excited and wanted to take it all in, every sight and smell.

There was a peaceful stillness filled only by the chirrups from a few sparrows. I could smell a light perfume coming from a nearby dryer vent. The air was calm and content, as was I. Smiling, just happy to be present, I stood by my car looking up at the clear blue vault-of-heaven sky.

I slowly took the steps, as Kathy had done so long ago, soaking in the space around me. It was a nicely kept older home with mature trees and well-trimmed bushes. As I neared the front door, I was delighted by the beautiful stained-glass door, with stunning sapphire letters, spelling "Welcome." It was amazing, with a bright floral pattern surrounded by grapevines. W-E-L-C-O-M-E. Each letter felt like a friendly handshake. I placed my hand flat on the glass, feeling the very door my mother had touched.

"Can I help you?" a man's voice asked from the other side of the door.

Startled, I moved my hand and stepped back as he opened the door.

"Oh, I'm very sorry to bother you, but I recently learned that my mother lived here for a while." I prattled on, "I heard about this door, and I guess I just wanted to touch something she had touched. I know it's crazy."

"Well, come on in."

"No, that's okay, but thanks. I don't want to be a bother."

"How long ago did your mom live here?" he asked, and motioned me to come in. "My name is Paul."

"Hi Paul, I'm Susan, it's nice to meet you. She lived here about forty-four years ago."

I entered the home and we stood in a simple entryway, just across from his office. His nameplate was on the wall next to the door, Paul Lanier, Office Manager. When I explained my story he had no idea this large brick home had once been a maternity home for young girls. However, he was sensitive to me as an adoptee, since his wife was adopted.

"She has been looking for her birth family for many years," he explained. "But they're from Korea and it's very difficult to get information."

"I can well imagine, but it is important to find your roots," I told him. "I thought I knew my roots, but I recently found out I was adopted."

"Your parents never told you that you were adopted? That's unforgivable," he offered. "I did read in the paper a few months back where this guy's whole life was a lie, and his folks made up reasons why they didn't have photos and so on. Turns out he was adopted."

"That's right; my adoptive mother had stories with an explanation for everything. But now that I know, I'm researching my birth mother. Which is how I got here, to this house. It used to be called Marcus House."

"Well, let me take you around so you can see where she lived. There's been one addition to the home, but the rest is the same. There are a few people in their rooms and we can't disturb them, but most everyone is in the TV room."

Both shocked and delighted, I followed Paul down the hallway. I'm usually concerned about what I touch, being a few colds shy of a germ-a-phobe, but here I touched everything. As we walked, I held out one hand feeling every bump and groove on the wall. Maybe she had felt the same imperfections.

"This is wonderful," I told Paul. "I do have a question though. My mother loved to draw and paint. She told her younger sister of an art room. Do you have any idea what room that might have been?"

"Well, there's one room with a skylight and lots of windows. It's not real big, and our residents seem to love to eat breakfast in there. Maybe that's it. We had it set up for cards and games, but no one uses it for that."

As we walked into the bright, freshly painted canary-yellow room, I hoped that this was the art room that she loved so much. I told Paul the story of how she focused on returning home for Christmas and painted many pictures of Christmastime.

"She actually left all her paintings tacked up in her room on the wall. She never got to come back and collect them. Her mother packed her things, picked her up at the hospital, and took her home in time for the family celebration on Christmas Eve."

"Oh, so it was all about the show for her mother? No one in the family knew she was pregnant?"

"Right." I explained while we walked to the next room, "The story was that Kathy, my birth mom, was away at college but then decided to drop out after the first semester. Her mother brought her home the day before the extended family arrived for Christmas."

"I hate to say it, but when I helped the agency get this place ready, we threw out everything we couldn't use. There was a lot of trash, old towels, sheets and rags, and sad to say—old paintings and drawings."

"Oh, I didn't expect to find anything of my mother's. Honestly I just wanted to see where she lived and the art room she loved."

"Okay, last stop on the tour, the TV room," Paul said as we peeked in.

It was a nice-sized room with a couch, several straight chairs, and three recliners. The elderly residents looked very comfortable while watching "The Price Is Right." With a few end tables, and a big coffee table in front of the couch, I could see it was a pleasant place to sit and watch, even argue and participate with the game show.

A small bald man with a big smile on his face said, "I'm glad they got rid of that Bob Barker fellow. Drew is much better."

There were two women sitting on a couch. One responded, "But Bob Barker was the real deal," and the other said, "This buffoon is always trying to be funny."

I smiled, remembering how much my mother had loved "The Price Is Right," and she also didn't like it when Bob Barker retired.

There were a few old movie posters on the wall and an old-time popcorn cart in the corner.

"Wow, that cart is great! Do you make a lot of popcorn?" I asked.

"We do. We have movie nights on Fridays and we do it up proper," Paul said with a smile. "Come check it out."

I followed him to the corner of the room, and it was indeed a fine popcorn machine, with a place to warm butter. There was a free-standing old wooden cabinet next to the cart. Paul opened it to reveal all the items needed for a fun Friday night. It was jam packed. On the top shelves were large sacks of corn. Boxes of salt filled the second shelf, and paper towels and bowls were squeezed in to fit at the bottom. Stacked underneath the cabinet were board games that anyone could play. I saw Sorry, Life, and my all-time favorite, Stratego, which I'd played with my brother when we were kids.

As I closed the cabinet doors, I heard something shake on the outside. I went around to the side, trying not to block Drew Carey on the TV. There was something hung on the side of the cabinet—it looked like a child's painting that had been framed. I lifted it off and took a closer look. It was a very old painting, about eight by ten inches. Some paint chips lay in the bottom of the frame.

Then I saw it was a painting of a Christmas tree.

"Oh my God!" I cried out. At the bottom were three letters, sort of run together, spelling out what looked like *KAY*.

"Is that...? No, it can't be... Is that one of your mother's paintings?" Paul asked.

"I think it is—I'm sure it is! She painted Christmas trees. That's what her mother told her to focus on, Christmas and gifts under the tree. *Only think about the Christmas tree at home.* And while she was here she went by the name 'Kay.'"

Sure enough, the painting was the same as had been described to me, with bells and stars decorating the bottom. Everything I'd learned about her story was true, right down to the painting of the Christmas tree. And there it was. forgotten on the side of an old cabinet.

"We always thought that belonged to a resident, our first resident," Paul said. "We assumed someone's grandchild painted it or something. You know, I remember seeing it the first Christmas, when we had this room decorated, and then I sort of forgot about it. It was the same time we got this cabinet. Someone must have hung it on the cabinet way back then."

"Any idea when that was, Paul?" I carefully put the picture back on its small nail, trying to suppress my feelings. Asking non-essential questions is my way of coping.

"No, but it had to be the same time we added on a storage room. For a while, we used several of these cabinets in the kitchen and laundry area, but then when we built the extra room we put the cabinets here and there. Let me go ask the house manager. She's been here since the beginning."

I went back to the entryway while Paul talked to the manager. I wondered, *Is there more? Is there any information about my mother's artwork?*

He returned after several minutes. "She said she remembers the painting. It was hung there on the cabinet to hide a big scratch is what she was told. She says it has always been there—not really sure where it came from."

"Well…Wow…Amazing," I managed to say. My voice cracked, and I fought back the tears.

"Hang on a second, I'll be right back." Paul walked away quickly as I wiped tears from my cheeks.

I thought, *He's sweet—he's getting me a tissue, but I want to get out of here!*

A minute later he returned, running towards me with something in his hand. "The manager said to give you the painting. Here you go." And he held it out to me. "I'm sure we can find something else to hide the scratch on the cabinet," he commented with a chuckle.

"Oh, I can have this painting?" I felt faint and had to sit down. "My mother's Christmas tree painting!" The well of emotion was incredible. I felt as if I were meeting my birth mother in person. I thought, *I have your painting, my first mom. I can feel you and I hope you can feel me.*

"Are you okay?" Paul asked. "You look a little pale."

"Paul, you don't know how much this means to me. Thank

you. I will never forget your kindness. Thank you from the bottom of my heart."

That did it—the rain shower of joy became uncontrollable. I thought about how much she must have loved me and it washed my soul. Oh, how I wish I could have met her, and thanked her for giving me life. How wonderful it would've been to tell her that I was all right. *I love you, my first mom.*

The very painting, my mother's painting that gave her solace during one of her darkest times; I now had it in my hands.

As I sit here today, a piece of Kathy is with me. I have my own solace now. I see it every day when I wake up and when I go to bed. And it's still incredible. The faded and flaked Christmas tree hangs in a new frame alongside my bed.

Thank you, Marcus House, for providing a safe haven for my mother and for not throwing away everything. Thank you, Sunland Springs, for being the caring museum for my mother's art, even if it was to simply hide a big scratch.

CHAPTER 12

Letters

"Letters are among the most significant memorials a person can leave behind."
— *Johann Wolfgang von Goethe*

ONE MORNING I WOKE UP EARLY; I don't often do that, but I had Mother on my mind. I sat up in bed and a familiar chill shot through me, creating a tumbling in my stomach. I realized it had been eight months since she left me. It was like a lever had dropped and shut off the main power. A menacing darkness returned.

I thought about my brother, Bob—how was he doing? So that morning, as soon as I was dressed, I sat down with a cup of coffee and wrote the following letter. I needed to write to him—to share my pain, but also to check in with him, a son who had also lost his mother.

Dear Bob.
It was eight months ago that our mother passed away, and it feels like forever since I've seen her or heard her voice. At the same time, it feels so recent that we were tag-teaming at her house, taking care of her. Like all the rest of the emotions involved, there are two sides or two conflicting feelings. I enjoyed my time with you but dreaded the ending, knowing it was Mom's passing that would bring closure of our time together.

I am thankful she didn't suffer more than she did. I am thankful she wasn't afraid or frantic the last couple of days. I am thankful she knew we loved her and we knew she loved us. I am thankful I had you to go through this with.

Often it's not the first emotion felt (this thankfulness), rather it's the final one held on to at the end of the day. Like the small soft pillow that helps us go to sleep, being thankful helps us get past the pain.

However, hate has been really creeping in on me lately. I don't really "hate" anything, but over these past months, that word has been said often.

I hate Wednesdays sometimes, especially if I find myself alone at some sort of store pondering should I buy this or that. Then to realize it's a Wednesday and she used to be with me, helping me along with such decisions. "Ugh…" I would say out loud. "I hate Wednesdays!" My heart would sink and tears would come, missing Mother. And, it wasn't the store or the item, neither meant anything — it was that time with her. Years of Wednesdays enjoying Mother is over.

She was so funny, you know? One time an unruly kid opened this box of weird cookies at TJ's and I saw her go back down the aisle a few moments later and grab a cookie. Or when she put this lovely smelling lotion all over her hands and arms, then on me… and it turned out to be luxury shower gel!

Sundays around 9 a.m. as I am getting up, I realize the day. I think of how it was your day with her and how you spent at least an hour chatting. I think about you and how you managed a few hours earlier. About a month after Mother passed away it dawned on me that you cannot replace that event, there's just no way to find something else to fill in for your time with her. Yeah, you can do other stuff, go on vacation, weed the yard, whatever…but you take the loss along with you. Sometimes it's easier, you may

*even forget for a while, but its there. I suppose it's under-
standable, but I hate that it's there for you, each Sunday
morning.*

*I hate that I have so much stuff I want to tell her. I
can't share pride or concern; she is no longer a phone call
away. We would spend hours being catty over her crazy
cat-lady neighbor or verbally rip-to-shreds the guy across
the street who'd let his dog leave presents in her yard. She
was very opinionated but always had something funny to
share.*

*Mother was truly part of everyday for me. If I didn't
talk to her, I thought about what she had going on that
day. She gave me a hard time for sleeping in and often
made goofy suggestions for things, not to mention the bizarre home remedies. But it was her way of being involved
in my life. Being there for her and trying to help also kept
me involved in her life as well. I know the same is true for
you. Yes, there was crap but we were all intertwined together. So, I hate it that it's so hard when one life is gone,
removed from our lives permanently. I know it's just how it
is, but some times, I really do hate it!*

*Which leads back around eventually to feeling grate-
ful for all the time, experiences (good and bad), and for our
faith in God and His plan for all of us. But nowhere in the
Bible does it say that I can't hate a few things along the
way, right? (Even if has been eight months.)*

*I love you Bob, you're my brother (always will be) and
I'm glad to have you on this journey.*

—Sue

I hoped he knew that this was my way of asking how he was doing.
'Fessing up to my feelings of hatred, and possibly validating any
feelings he may have had about Sunday mornings.

I'm a frequent letter writer, especially since Mother passed
away. When things settled enough, I reached out to everyone
Mom had been in contact with over the years: her very best

friends, family in the U.S., and Welsh relatives abroad. I explained her illness, death, and the love she felt for them, but then asked if they knew I was adopted. Did they have any information for me?

Letter after letter was answered, and most of them said the same thing: "I had no idea your mom adopted you."

One response that was different came as an email from a family member. When I expressed my desire to search for my birth mother, he seemed to berate me, as if it somehow diminished who my mother was. Later, when I emailed explaining that I'd found my birth mom but that she was deceased, the writer suggested that this was in fact a positive outcome. "Possibly, she was a bitch from hell," he wrote. Possibly, someone with so little sensitivity would never hear from me again.

My mother's second cousin wrote, "Your folks had been living in the White Mountains and we just didn't have a lot of contact. Then when you were about six months old your mom phoned and explained all that had been going on up north with building cabins and all the snow. With excitement in her voice, she was pleased to announce that she also had a baby girl and they were back down in the valley to stay."

Jean, my mother's oldest and dearest friend, didn't respond to two letters. I hoped that she was taking her time, but I also wondered if she was upset. She would have gotten the small note that Cathy helped Mother write explaining her illness, and then within a month received my letter explaining that she had passed. Mother's death may have deeply affected Jean, since they had been friends since high school, but I had no way of knowing.

It wasn't until late summer, about eleven months after Mother passed away, that I heard from Jean. I pulled up to the mailbox, got out of the car and grabbed the mail. I sat back down and flipped through a few bills and sales circulars, and there it was! Here's what she wrote:

Dear Susan,
I've never been known as "a woman of few words," but be-

lieve me, I am now! I am having a very hard time accepting the sad news of your mother's passing.

I thank God that she had a beautiful caring family and a dear friend, Cathy, to be near in her final weeks of life. Oh how I wish I could have been there to help in any way, even if just to give comfort to your mom by holding her hand.

I will surely miss her letters and the enjoyment of our life-long friendship.

I did know that you were adopted and promised your mother to keep her secret. We never spoke of the situation and I respected her wishes. The one and only time she gave me any details was before she got you, she wrote me a letter explaining.

Susan, I have fought with the idea of breaking my promise for months now. I have talked to your mom many nights in a row asking her what I should do.

"Glenys, are you there? Please, your daughter is asking me what I know about her adoption and I don't know what to do. I know I promised to keep the secret, but she knows and she really wants my help. Glenys, should I help your daughter?"

I think my husband was beginning to wonder if I had lost it, talking to the ceiling so much. He was the one to suggest that I follow my heart and just make a decision — tell you or keep quiet and move on.

I decided that it was no longer a secret, the cat's out of the bag, and my dear friend would want me to help you. After all, you cannot put the cat back in the bag so we may as well move forward.

May your mom and God forgive me if this is the wrong thing, but I've enclosed her correspondence to me when she first found out about getting you. The letter is very old, but it touched me so that I kept it all these years in an old journal from that year, 1964.

I hope this helps you find what you're looking for,

146   *Late Discoveries*

Susan. Please know, from my heart to yours, your mother loved you very much and she felt the secret was best for you. She wanted you to feel the same as Bobby and that she and your dad were a typical family with two kids, a boy and a girl.

I do apologize for taking close to a year to share this with you, but as I've explained, I was in such torment with this difficult decision.

Sincerely,

Jean

I sat in my car right in front of the mailbox, reading her letter. Before opening it, I assumed it would be a note explaining that she had been traveling or moving or something. But here it was, finally—the break I'd been hoping for. Her oldest and dearest friend knew about me...she knew I was adopted. In her own words, I had a letter from my mother explaining where I came from.

I pulled out a small envelope—the edges yellowed, ink softened—and recognized my mother's handwriting. Indeed, she had sent Jean a letter, and now, forty-four years later, I sat holding it. It was worn soft with age and pressed flat, probably from being stored in a tight space between other pages. Possibly everything I could want to know was folded neatly on these pages, written by my mother's hand. Would she have ever imagined that one day I too would read this letter with all its secrets? I am sure she did not—this was a unique situation in which a very special woman felt compelled to offer me this small envelope of paradise in hopes of providing some peace.

The paper of the envelope was smooth and fine between my fingers. I was almost afraid to open it to remove the letter, but I lifted the flap and slid it out. I unfolded the sheets, four pages of tan paper, an old-fashioned stationary with her initials GLW at the bottom. I had never seen this paper, but her writing was deeply familiar. Through my tears I read my mother's own words to her longtime friend.

My dearest Jean,

We have such excitement at our house right now and before things get very busy I had to write to you my dear.

I am sure you noticed on the envelope that we have a new address in Phoenix. Yes, we have just settled in from the White Mountains to a small apartment in town. Bobby is especially happy since we've arrived in time for Halloween and he expects to clean up with candy in our new neighborhood.

Jean, I am only sharing this with one person—YOU! I ask that you keep this matter private and never speak about it to anyone. Yes, like in school I am asking that you keep my secrets. Ha ha.

A couple of months ago Rob told me about speaking with a nice family from the valley; we had rented our cabins to them in the past.

He said, "You remember Glen, the Bardlows, with all the kids?" And I did remember, but we hadn't seen them in a while, since we sold the Broken Arrow Lodge. Well, Rob said, "Mr. Bardlow told me that his daughter, the one just out of high school, was pregnant and giving up the baby."

Jean, I hope you are sitting down....we are going to adopt that baby! Can you believe it, after all this time?

About a month ago, his daughter, Kathy, went to live in Tucson and she will have the baby there. They met with the staff at the adoption agency telling them they couldn't keep the baby and needed help with arrangements. The Bardlows have requested us as the placement and after a few phone calls and paperwork—we've got the green light!

We must be ready though; the baby could come early with the mother being young and such a slight gal. So, we are in the apartment getting ready for the baby. She is due in December so we only have a month and the agency needs to visit us once we are settled.

I tell you Jean, this baby is as much for my mom as anyone. She is over the moon with excitement for this little

*one. We were with an agency years ago when Bobby was
little but there weren't any babies for us. I think it was our
age, but this time with knowing the family, this baby is
ours. I guess you could say the baby is earmarked for us.*

*Jean, we have a plan and a story and no one will know
that this little boy or girl was adopted. We are telling everyone that I had the baby. Mom doesn't want the child to feel
any different than Bobby growing up. She says, "This is a
Godsend, Glen, we're getting our baby and Bobby won't
grow up alone, as you did."*

*Please, dear friend, mum's the word and thank you for
keeping our little secret.*

Love love love you my dear,
Glenys
P.S. Pictures to come of our little cherub.

How phenomenal, my mother's letter describing her anticipation
for me! I drove the short block home, pulling in the driveway
filled with the excitement of my new information. I had often
wondered how a couple their ages managed to adopt a newborn
without special circumstances, or without knowing the mother.
Now it's clear, they *did* know my birth mother and her family.

I was still a bit disappointed by the lack of information about
my father. There was not one mention of his name or the circumstances surrounding the pregnancy.

The warmth of my mother's words describing my grandmother's love and wishes to adopt made me feel giddy and outweighed
any concern for my birth father's identity. I had adored my grandmother and felt her love for me every moment she was alive. Now
I had written proof of her desire for me, before she had even held
me. How lovely. How satisfying.

Again, I concede I may never find out who my birth father
was—or still is, for that matter. Of course, like my birth mother,
he may also be deceased.

Opening the mailbox that day and getting Jean's letter was

wonderful. Then, seeing my mother's letter I felt like an archae-ologist with the find of a lifetime. As letters have gone out and come in, explaining feelings and sharing information, there will never be a more special letter than the one from my mother to her best friend. I'm so thankful for Jean's decision to share such a magnificent gift.

CHAPTER 13

The White Purse

"This is not a letter but my arms around you for a
brief moment."
                                —Katherine Mansfield

EACH DAY WHILE PREPARING to go out into the world, I see my
mother's purse; a lighthouse beacon determined to catch my
attention with its bright, focused beam. This was her favorite
white purse. She used it over the past decade during the summer months, and it was her last purse during her final months. It
accompanied her to the doctor's office for her check-ups, it went
to my brother's house for a final visit, and it made the trip to the
imaging center where she had her final tests done. I am unable
to see it for what it is—a simple white handbag. All I can see in
the white purse is my mother, and all I can feel is the pain of loss
in my heart.

Mother's purse held, among other things, the last letter from
her granddaughter. She had not gotten to read it. I wonder if Ashleigh ever considered that her letter might go unopened because
it arrived too late.

I remember the day the letter arrived. My mother had no
strength and was unable to even stay awake as I tried to explain
that she had mail. So the letter went into her purse, which always
stood alongside the couch right next to her, in case there was
an alert moment for me to read to her. Unfortunately, the letter
quickly became "out of sight, out of mind." My poor mother's

house was overrun with nurses and family members, her living room taken over by the large hospital bed she was confined to, not to mention the cords and tubes and the oxygen tank and other assorted medical supplies. I was so focused on just trying to be with my mother in her last days that the letter from my daughter was buried under heaps of responsibilities, worries, and grief.

Feeling brave, I finally opened it—the letter from Ashleigh, Mother's only granddaughter.

Dear Gram,

I keep thinking about all the things we used to do together in Payson. The more I think about it, the more I worry that we took it for granted, that every summer we would get to go to Payson and spend a week with you, playing games and watching movies and eating ice cream and getting those huge rectangle pizzas from Domino's. I hope you know that I really appreciated spending time with you and I loved every minute of our little vacations together. Remember basketball in the back yard and rollerblading at the park? And fishing at the pond, which was hysterical! (What good, good times we had.)

I love you so very much Gram and it really kills me to see you having to go through something like this. I guess I just thought you were going to live forever, you've been healthy as a horse and you seemed invincible to me. I wish I could trade bodies with you for a while, just to give you a break.

I feel so badly that our time together has been short and far between for these past few years. If I could do it all over again I would make sure to see you all the time. For that, I am sorry. I'm sorry I didn't see you more, I'm sorry I didn't tell you that I love you more. I'm sorry I didn't kiss and hug you more. I'm going to miss you so much, I hope you know that?

You know, I've been thinking about what we were all

talking about this last Sunday, about what happens to you after you die. I kind of agree with you, I don't understand how everyone who has passed away is up there in the sky, just milling around. I don't really know what to think, but I do know for sure that dying isn't the end. I'm not sure how I'm so certain of that, but I really am. I know that just because someone dies doesn't mean I'll never see them again, never be around them or talk to them again, but I don't think they're really standing up there in heaven, waiting around for me to die and join them. Doesn't the idea of eternal life exhaust you? It exhausts me and I'm only 21.

I think that people live on in their loved ones. People's memories live on in the people they left on earth. You have touched so many lives, Gram, and I know that whenever I'm around Mom and she's watering plants and singing to herself that it's you, telling me you love and miss me. I know that whenever I see a traditional tea cup full of tea, I remember you showing Hayden and me how to read tea leaves. Anytime I think about sitting at the table in the very early morning hours I think about having cereal in Payson while you drink tea and do the crossword puzzle. In fact, the beautiful hours in the morning always remind me of you. It's my favorite time of the day. There are so many things that make me think of you, sometimes it is overwhelming.

So, whenever the sun rises and floods the sky in beautiful light pastel colors, I will think of my favorite Gram and how much she means to me. Whenever I have a cup of tea, I will let its warmth fill me with love, just like you have done. Whenever I see a crossword puzzle in the newspaper, I will try to do it but maybe you could give a little help every once in a while? You always were better at those than me!

I love you so much and I'm thinking of you right now as I type this and I hope you're snug in your bed dreaming peacefully. I'll think of you when I get up in the morning

and hope you're having a good day. Whenever I feel sad,
I tell myself that I shouldn't feel sad because I get to see
you again in less than two weeks! In less than two weeks I
can wrap my arms around you and kiss you and hug you
and tell you how much I love you. Until then, I'll just keep
writing you letters.
   Love Always,
   Your Ashleigh

My initial reaction was *this is a huge mistake! Run!* I was sitting at
the kitchen table in our bright breakfast nook, and by the end of
the letter, my head throbbed from the blinding light. The silence
in the room made the words scream in my ears, and my heart
ached. I folded the letter back up, put it away, and walked outside. Honestly, I felt like walking to the corner and right in front
of the biggest truck I could see. I hurt so bad.

It was too much for me to take. The precious love between
my mother and my daughter was obvious, and all I could think
of was *my mother didn't get to hear these lovely words.* I was over-
whelmed with sadness at the loss we all experienced the day my
mother passed away. And acutely aware of what Ashleigh was feeling when she wrote the letter.

My daughter was writing a letter every day toward the end of
my mother's life and was planning another trip to visit soon. Little
did she know when she wrote this one that she would never get to
see her grandmother in this life again.

I know in my soul that this letter belongs in that white purse,
even though my mother won't ever dig through it again.

The purse was a key component in her life, "Can't go anywhere without the purse," she'd always tell me.

Mother's purse held needed items: an extra pair of clip-on
earrings, a few toothpicks in plastic, and a large book of coupons.
But the treasure was her wallet, with its secret compartments
overflowing with photographs. Mother had several pictures of her
parents from over the years, along with sweet inscriptions on the
back, such as *My lovely Mum.* Most of all, Mother had fifteen

pictures of her four grandkids, ready to share with anyone interested—and even those who weren't!

However, in three separate places within her wallet I found
scraps of mysterious white paper with tiny printing. One was in a
picture sleeve, the second in the change compartment, and the
last in another zippered compartment. Each paper had the same
typewritten paragraph:

*Dear friends, please do not set limits on my grief. Neither
my love nor the depths of my sorrow can be measured. I am
unable to heal on a timetable set by another. Weeks and
months have no meaning when set against the measure of
my love. Walk with me please, this difficult road of recovery, I promise you I indeed will heal, when I have grieved
enough for me.*

In going through her belongings after her death, I found at least
twenty-five copies of that little paper. They were collected from
all over the house—in the laundry room, tacked onto corkboards,
tucked into picture frames, in her desk and end table drawers,
and most likely a number of other places I didn't find. I even
found the original paper, which was given to my mother after my
grandmother passed away. This was a reminder, and something
she could share with others confounded by the depth of grief.

Looking at this message hidden in her wallet, I felt a renewed
sense of understanding. I was holding onto a piece of her that
had remained walled off from me. In her attempts to protect my
brother and me, she had prevented us from knowing that part of
her.

I can see that the grief she felt after losing her mom was unbearable and it changed her. Then, in the blink of an eye her dad
passed away. Yes, she forged ahead and days and weeks passed,
but her spirit was shadowed with a dark veil of loss and she held
tightly to those small pieces of paper.

Fifteen years went by and then her husband passed away, but
she still had those squares of paper to help get her through the

pain. Mother's loneliness was one of her biggest challenges, but it was always secondary to the loss of her parents.

Now that I have lost her, I can begin to understand what she was going through when her parents passed away. We all feel loss and handle grief differently. For me each time I enter my closet, the purse draws my gaze like an irresistible magnetic force.

Even when I've forgotten about the purse, and I'm thinking about which pair of shoes to wear, my soul knows it's there well before I glance up and see it on the shelf. It's been a challenge for me to figure out what to do with this personal item, Mother's constant companion. It lived on a table in the entryway for a few days, but seeing it all the time was just too upsetting. I moved it to our rarely used couch in the den, and it quickly accumulated more of Mother's things on top of it, but that darned purse still found me every time I passed through the room. Eventually everything was put in an appropriate place and Mother's purse took up residence in my closet. It's been there quite some time now. We have reached an understanding, the purse and I. It stands as a symbol of the commitment and love I received from my mother, and I know it is my responsibility never to forget what she did for me or who she was. I've realized that I can't move Mother's purse, I can't get rid of it, and it's impossible even to hide it somewhere. It was part of her, with her all the time, and to do something with it would feel like I'd be doing something with her. The last thing I want to do is hide or banish my mother from my life.

Sometimes the "purse reminders" get me down and I must deal with the loss of my mother, the knowledge of my adoption, and the secrecy. The emotional anguish is heavy on some days, and like the purse, I'm challenged to move away from it. It seems that I carry my mother with me always, very much like a purse, slung closely around me and comfortable—most of the time. But every once in a while, it feels like there are bricks in there, and the strap digs into my shoulder while the purse threatens to crack my ribs if it swings too much—but that's life. More and more, my anguish, my "purse," is part of my body and I don't notice so much that it's there or that she is there. We are sort of "one" together for the rest of my journey and I embrace the purse. I embrace *her* for being my mother.

The day will surely come when I can get what I need from the closet and just close the door, Mother's purse safely inside as simply one of many objects on a shelf. On that day the purse won't carry so much weight in my heart because my mother's memory and love is truly not a burden, but a gift that will live on inside me for all time.

CHAPTER 14

My Dad

"To a father growing old nothing is dearer than a daughter."

— *Euripides*

MY ADOPTIVE DAD, Robert, passed away one month after I turned nineteen. He had a brief battle with cancer, and lost the fight when he was just sixty-five. Although I really didn't know him as an adult, many people liked him and said he had the gift of gab.

One of my favorite memories was watching my dad, my brother, and my nephew pose for a family picture by sitting on each other's laps. Dad was at the bottom, then Bob, and my young nephew Daniel on the top. Dad could not stop laughing—he was cracking up. He'd stop for a few breaths and then start again. I suppose a funny guy-thing happened, and I didn't know what, but I laughed along. He was very sweet with his grandsons and I know he would have loved my kids, as well. I wish I had known my dad longer, but his time on this earth was short and it was not meant to be. Since his death, I have been without a father, until now.

I have a birth dad. He has my blue eyes and he has my daughter's ears, small and perfect. He used to have sandy colored hair but it's now gray, trimmed short and neat. He is creative in so many ways and is more concerned with sharing his gifts than with business. He worked at the things he loved instinctively, and the money came. To say he is successful is an understatement.

Over the years, he has owned dozens of horses. Just like my daughter, Ashleigh, the bond with his equine friends is exceptional. At this moment, we both have five dogs—which is hysterical to me. I mean, *who has five dogs?* He is an amateur photographer who loves to sketch and paint, but made his fortune as a writer. Together, we laugh easily, enjoy nature, movies, but most of all children. I'm surprised we never met while I was volunteering at a local children's charity.

My birth dad has a keen physical resemblance to my son, his grandson, Hayden. Their similarities are face shape, hands and feet, height, and best of all, their sense of humor. I can well imagine Hayden looking exactly like my birth dad when he's older. They are equal in height and both played volleyball in high school. *How incredible for Hayden to see someone who looks just like him,* I muse. To know that they both want to go down to our local tattoo shop, Black Lotus, and get the same tattoo fills me with giddy happiness. And I don't even like tattoos.

This man is truly the missing link in my life that may remain forever in my dreams and child-like heart. He is a bright figment of an adult orphan's imagination, nameless and without flesh-and-blood form. This dad lives in my mind, delightfully perfect.

Only his first name was provided to the adoption agency that placed me; however, it was redacted on the paperwork I received. I pleaded with the agency in person, with someone behind the front desk, and then finally on the phone with an assistant director.

"Please, is there any way you can just tell me what my birth dad's name is?" I begged.

"Legally we cannot give you that information. Besides, we don't have his first and last name, only a first name was provided by your birth mother," she explained.

"Maybe you could tell me some of the boys' names in your family, and the last one will be my dad's name," I sheepishly suggested.

"Well, all I can tell you is that his name is a very common name."

As I tried to define common, she laughed and said, "I am *so* sorry I cannot tell you."

Well, I'm sorry too, but keeping his first name protected is ridiculous, especially since it's a common name. It would mean something to me, whether it's Tom, John, Bill, or Ted; I would know my birth father's name.

I began my quest to find him by asking every newfound family member, even suggesting ways of helping them remember. "Maybe if you look at a few old pictures of Kathy from her high school days you will remember? Try and think of when they spent time together, did he come to your parents' house? They would have dated her senior year in high school and I had to be conceived in March of 1964. Maybe they did something that year for Valentine's Day. *Think*—who was around?"

"It was such a long time ago, I don't remember a guy at all," said her younger sister. All the answers were the same; no one remembered whom she dated. No one had a clue whom she planned to marry after learning she was pregnant. It's as if it had never happened.

The non-identifying information I obtained from the adoption agency said he was twenty years old at the time of the paperwork, good looking, with blue eyes and sandy brown hair, and over six feet tall. He weighed 185 pounds and was in good physical condition. He worked at an auto paint shop at the time I was born. *But had he just turned twenty, or was he close to twenty-one?*

I joined the class reunion Web site of my birth mother's high school class, searching for 1964 graduates of North High School who might have known her. The posting was unusual, but it got the point across.

I passed away in 1999, but my daughter, whom I gave up for adoption right after high school, is seeking to know me better through friends, and possibly her birth dad.

> *Susan, Kathy's daughter, has joined this site in her memory.*
>
> *Did you know Kathy? I am her daughter, Susan, and I'm forty-four now; married with two grown kids. I truly don't "need" anything, just info or stories about my mom (or if you know who my dad is, that'd be awesome.)*
>
> *Thanks so much if you can help!*

At first, it was so exciting and there were many responses from Kathy's classmates, but although they recalled seeing her, they did not recollect her personally, nor could they think of any friends.

One classmate said, "I remember her, she was so pretty and tall, but we didn't run in the same circles. Sorry."

Anyone who thought they might have remembered her at all got an extra note from me trying to prod their memory. Could they recall anything, any friend, or any detail about her from high school?

Weeks and months went by without any further response to my post as Kathy. It dawned on me that my birth dad was twenty years old at the time I was born; he might have already graduated high school. Most people graduate at eighteen, so maybe... I posted the same information on the graduating class of 1963's page, and 1962's page, hoping for the best. Not one person responded. This was another dead end without much to go on, leaving no other options. I guess it's possible that he had dropped out of high school, and that's why no one remembered him. But where did he meet Kathy, and what was their story?

I've thought about him often, trying to envision what he looked like back then. While looking through online high school reunion pages, I noted how the men looked now in their mid-sixties, and wondered how my dad had aged. *Does he have a big family? Is he married or divorced?* Several were already retired and enjoying their freedom and hobbies. *Is my dad retired?* Whoever he is, whatever choices he has made, I would very much enjoy knowing him and seeing a picture of him, with no expectations.

Has my dad thought of Kathy along the way, or of the child they conceived?

After my long journey of discovery, there are many questions left unanswered. It's possible they'll never be answered. However, there *is* another dad in addition to my adopted dad. Biologically, I belong to someone else and I carry his DNA. My birth dad is part of me, whether or not I know his story or even his first name.

CHAPTER 15

Dreams

"The future belongs to those who believe in the beauty of their dreams."
                                                           —*Eleanor Roosevelt*

IN THE PAST YEAR, I've dreamt about my mother often. They've been about various circumstances—the two of us at the movies, or discussing her dog Petey, her being mad at me, and even one where we discussed her moving, which she'd done five years ago.

"Damn you!" she yelled. "I'm not moving into a place that's flat on the ground!"

The dream was vivid, as most of them are, and her anger apparent. Mother liked living in the trailer home she'd spent thirty-five years in; she was three feet off the ground and had come to feel a certain amount of safety. The home she moved to in the retirement community was very nice, but level with the ground.

"Why are you making me do this? Damn it, I'm not going to go, even if your brother tries to carry me!" (When she was alive we'd threaten—mostly as a joke—that Bob would carry her.)

On our last vacation together, Mother, my brother, and I with our spouses, Rosanna and Mike, and Rosanna's dad Joe, vacationed for ten days in paradise—Maui. One night not long ago I slipped back to that beautiful place. In my dream, we were walking on the beach, Mother holding my arm for support.

She said, "Oh this is great for my tired, aching feet."

"Ahh yes, it's nice and cool when the water splashes up," I agreed.

"Don't get me wrong, Sue, I love her—but that Rosanna is a tenacious shopper. We spent a good four hours shopping, covering every square inch of those market stores. She looked at everything, a few things twice—I thought my bloody feet would burst!"

"Oh, they really must be sore."

Then in a serious tone she ordered, "Go and get your brother to carry me." She smiled and said, "Tell him I'll buy him a beach ball."

We both laughed for a few moments. She had such a quirky sense of humor, even in my dreams.

For as long as I can recall, Mom always joked with Bob that if he did this or that for her, she'd be sure to get him a beach ball. So whenever Mother asked him what he wanted for Christmas, he'd answer, "A beach ball." And when he turned forty, she didn't even have to ask, she just showed up with a big, brightly colored red, blue, and green beach ball. So it's not surprising—in fact it was quite pleasant—that in my dream she'd joke with Bob about a beach ball.

When she's kind or funny, the dreams are enjoyable. When she's mad at me, I tell her she's being mean, and not to talk to me that way. I've gotten used to the dreams, as much as one can. I've learned to be present, realizing that I'm dreaming. Bringing in my logical mind provides some control, so that I feel safe and know that it's just a dream—until the night that it *wasn't*.

Mother had been gone almost a year and I *was not* thinking about her. Mike was on the couch with a recently broken collarbone, and I was alone in bed, knitting, then praying, and nicely falling asleep. But this time I drifted off into the most realistic dream I have ever had. It was so vivid and so clear that I was sure it was real. And when I woke up around three a.m., I wasn't confused or frustrated, but felt as if I'd just spent time with my mother.

My very first thought was, *Dang, I didn't ask her any adoption questions.* But, it was so nice to see her—I felt as if I'd just had this little visit, and then I was back home. I felt peacefully calm. I turned over and went right back to sleep. It was the briefest waking moment between dreams that I've ever had. And when I woke up the next morning, I didn't think about the dream.

I got up and joined Mike in the kitchen. He always gives me a hug and asks how I slept. Normally, I tell him about my crazy dreams and we get on with our morning and coffee, etc. But suddenly, I remembered. The entire dream and all the details came rushing over me like Niagara Falls. I was anything but calm as I shared my captivating dream, which was more like an out-of-body experience.

"I was walking up a path in the White Mountains. Small cinders, reddish stones, crunched under my feet. I looked at the ground, up at the few scrub trees, and then over to the end of the path. There, painted bright goldenrod by rays of the sun, was a house with wide welcoming steps leading up to the porch. It was creamy tan with chocolate brown trim, and large stones surrounded the fireplace chimney. It was a very nice place with big pine trees all around the property. The entire home came into view as I walked up the path, where it turned into a circle driveway. The house was on my right, and as I looked to the left, I noticed a white painted picnic table and people sitting in chairs. Two ladies wearing dresses were sitting in the chairs and a man sat on the bench. He was leaning forward with his elbows resting on his knees. He looked very familiar.

"As I approached, I could see that it was my mother and grandparents! My heart bounced and I gasped—the sight took my breath away. My grandfather, my Grampie, looking just as I remember him in his khaki pants and muted plaid button-up shirt, leaning over and sitting casually.

"He stood up and walked over to Mom, my grandmother, and said, 'Let's go, Dor.' Oh I remember how he always used to call her Dor.

"I looked over at her, my beloved grandmother, who meant so much to me when I was a child. She was beautiful in her soft pink dress with her hair done up. She focused solely on my grandfather and walked away with him towards the house. I wondered if she even saw me.

"Then my eyes were drawn to my mother. She sat in a metal-framed chair with colored webbing, the old kind we used to have on the patio. Mother's dress was a pale yellow with a fine blue stripe. She was beautiful. As I walked nearer, I could see her hair with its famous wave at the front. It was shining, beautiful auburn with gold highlights. I couldn't get over how great she looked! Her eyes were like bright blue pools just gleaming at me. She smiled, so happy to see me, and I could feel her love.

"'There's my girl,' she said. Her face was full and glowing.

"I felt happiness all around me, from her and my grandparents and the magical place itself. The scene glistened as I looked through my tears; it was stunningly bright. All I could do was weep as I walked right up in front of her. She reached out for my hands, taking them in hers.

"'So how are you? What have you been up to?' Her tone was playful. She'd asked me that a thousand times, the same way. She was obviously very happy. Things were different, with her in this place. This wasn't her being sick or dying, and yet it was real. The radiant light around her filled me with a warmth I'd never felt before.

"But suddenly confusion began to intrude—I knew Mother had passed away but there we were.

"I felt a familiar pain growing inside. *Does she know she passed away?*

"Her tone was much like a Wednesday morning when I would visit her for the day. I didn't feel as light-hearted as she clearly did. I needed to tell her what had happened. I began to cry and spoke softly to her.

"'Mom, you're not with me any more!' I stood sobbing and shaking. My heart was breaking again. 'You died, Mom.'

"'Oh now, shhhh, shhhh, it's okay, I know…I know,' she said. With her calm smile, she comforted me. She knew what was real and instantly knew my heart. She held my hands in her left hand, and placed her right hand on top.

"'It's okay sweetie, it's okay.' She patted my hand and said it again and again.

"I felt like a child, a sad little girl. 'But Mom, I can't talk to you anymore, or see you and ask you about things… and we don't have our Wednesdays. Oh, how I miss you! I just don't know what to do.' I felt the real pain of her loss, and my heart was crushed.

"She never got up. She simply held my hands calmly, looked right into my eyes, and instructed, 'You go on with your life.'

"Plain, common advice in a reassuring tone—but it was so much more. It was my mother understanding me and sharing with me, soul to soul."

As I told my husband about the experience, I cried and could hardly get the words out. Sobbing in his arms, probably more than when she had passed away, I tried to explain the tenderness, but most of all how real the dream felt.

"Mike, she smiled at me and I felt her love and tenderness as my mother, and I smiled back at her. Unbelievably, I was calm and stopped crying. Then I looked down and took a step back, and our hands released from one another. It was like a sudden jerking motion—I was pulled up into the sky. It was the opposite of falling but with the same frightful feeling in my stomach. I felt disoriented and I was pulled farther away from her. She was only a blur, and then it was all gone—the house, my grandparents, and her smiling face. The dream was over."

Mike hugged me tightly. "Wow," he said. "That is incredible. What do you think you meant when you told her that you didn't know what to do?"

"I have no idea. I hadn't been thinking about Mother or *not knowing what to do*, whatever that means. I've thought about trying to figure out who my dad was, or is, but that's about it. Maybe it's my subconscious. But I have to say, her answer and holding my hands that way means the world to me, and it always will—dream or not."

We held each other in a close embrace and I felt safe and loved, but also a bit confused. I suspected this dream had more to it and I continued to wonder what it all meant.

When I began my road to discovery after Mother passed away, a small voice in my head told me that I should write about it—write about her life, my life, and my family's biggest secret. I was full of anticipation and excitement. After years of wishing and thinking *Someday I want to write a book*, I finally had my story.

When I began, I first made an outline and started to write. It went along well, writing itself actually. But, before long I slowed down and stopped. I had no idea how to end my story without making myself feel even worse for telling it. A tale like this can easily be sorrowful, and it needs a great, uplifting finale. But it wasn't here—there was no newfound family waiting for me, and there was no storybook ending. I prepared to tell my friends and family that I was quitting; I simply couldn't do it. I didn't want to do it.

Then that night, during a lovely, super-real experience that was something beyond a dream, my mother gave me the answer, in more ways than one.

Although the words she said were simple, what she advised me to do was to pick myself up out of the mud, hose off, and *just do it*. It was pure, brave, loving encouragement. And I heard her—no more wallowing in self-pity or despair, no waffling back and forth between cowardice and confidence—just do it.

Yes, Mother, I did it! I'm going on with my life, believing in my dreams.

I Am

I AM FOREVER SOFTENED by the forced reflection that comes with loss.

I am forever lonesome because a special relationship is gone.

I am forever changed by the knowledge of my history and my beginnings. The soulful emotion from a time the mind cannot remember is the foundation of life.

I am forever comforted by God and my faith in His plan which guides me to each new day. In John 8:32, He said "You shall know the truth and the truth shall make you free."

I am forever inspired by the knowledge that all adopted or fostered children are incredible gifts from God. They also have remarkable beginnings and stories. And each is no less a child, no less a gift, and no less incredible.

Yes, I am a Late Discovery Adoptee. This means simply that I discovered later in life that I was adopted. These things happened to me, making them part of my story, but it's not who I am. It has changed my life and given me new purpose; for that, I am very thankful.

Acknowledgments

I am here because two women loved me. My birth mom who brought me into this world, and my mother who deeply loved me, and gave me the world—a family.

I dedicate this book to Ashleigh and Hayden, the most precious people in my life. The moment each was born I felt humbled, realizing that part of the reason for my existence was for their existence. You both are incredibly unique, yet similar in that you have such special gifts and abilities. From the beginning, having you made me a better person, and I love you both, to the moon and back.

This book happened because of my fearless supporter and soulmate, Mike. Thank you for hanging in there; I love you forever. You and your family have shaped me as much as my own.

Always in my heart is my brother, Bob. Without him, I wouldn't be who I am. He helped form my childhood, and has always been a force in my life, even if he didn't know it. I love you and Rosanna, and your family.

Thank you, special friends at Search Triad, for making me feel like I fit in. Especially to Emelin, who reached out to me and helped me to feel not so alone. As a group, Search Triad gave me validation, support, and love that helped me find my courage. I wish everyone affected by adoption could have the comfort you've given me.

American Adoption Congress, my home away from home, has empowered me to become more involved on a national level. At my first AAC conference, I learned that adoption is about addition and not subtraction. This is so true! Thank you, new friends and fellow board members, for welcoming me with open arms.

Together, I hope we will change laws so that every adoptee in every state may have their Original Birth Certificate.

A special thanks to Shelley Fleming for her editing expertise. In addition, I extend great appreciation to my favorite RN-sister-in-law, Stephanie Albers, for help with final review and edits. But most of all, I thank the person who has worked on this probably as much as I have, my daughter Ashleigh. Your reads and re-reads, suggestions, encouragement when it was too sad, and your writer's mind have been a tremendous strength for me. I deeply appreciate the help you and Teri gave me, every step of the way.

I thank God for the journey, the roller coaster ride, and it's through my faith that I can see and feel the purpose of my life.

Resources

For more information on adoption or searching

www.americanadoptioncongress.org
Committed to adoption reform, the AAC promotes honesty, openness, and respect for family connections in adoption, foster care, and assisted reproduction. The AAC has an online group to discuss legislation and offer personal support, which includes late discovery adoptees (LDAs).

www.searchtriad.org
A local Arizona search-and-support group for anyone in the adoption triad. This group helped me in unimaginable ways. Check for local Search Triad support groups in your area.

www.isrr.net
International Soundex Reunion Registry is the first important step of any search. It is the largest, oldest, and most respected mutual consent registry in the world.

www.almasociety.org
Adoptees' Liberty Movement Association is the pioneer organization in fighting for the rights of adoptees everywhere and is the oldest comprehensive registry of its kind.

www.adoptioninstitute.org
The Evan B. Donaldson Adoption Institute provides leadership that improves adoption laws, policies, and practices—through sound research, education and advocacy—in order to better the lives of everyone touched by adoption.

www.latediscovery.org
Information, stories, and online support dealing specifically with being a Late Discovery Adoptee.